SUCCESSFUL
TALENT
STRATEGIES

SUCCESSFUL
TALENT
STRATEGIES

ACHIEVING SUPERIOR BUSINESS RESULTS
THROUGH MARKET-FOCUSED STAFFING

DAVID SEARS

AMACOM
American Management Association
New York • Atlanta • Brussels • Buenos Aires • Chicago • London • Mexico City
San Francisco • Shanghai • Tokyo • Toronto • Washington, D.C.

Special discounts on bulk quantities of AMACOM books are available to corporations, professional associations, and other organizations. For details, contact Special Sales Department, AMACOM, a division of American Management Association, 1601 Broadway, New York, NY 10019.
Tel.: 212-903-8316. Fax: 212-903-8083.
Web site: www.amacombooks.org

This publication is designed to provide accurate and authoritative information in regard to the subject matter covered. It is sold with the understanding that the publisher is not engaged in rendering legal, accounting, or other professional service. If legal advice or other expert assistance is required, the services of a competent professional person should be sought.

Library of Congress Cataloging-in-Publication Data

Sears, David, 1947–
    Successful talent strategies : achieving superior business results through market-focused staffing / David Sears.
        p.   cm.
    Includes index.
    ISBN 0-8144-0746-3 (hardcover)
    1. Employees—Recruiting.   2. Employee selection.   3. Employee retention.   4. Strategic planning.   5. Personnel management.   I. Title.

HF5549.5.R44   S43   2003
658.3'11—dc21   2002007239

Printing number

10   9   8   7   6   5   4   3   2   1

For Mary and Jennie

☑ CONTENTS

PART I TALENT STRATEGIES ARE BUSINESS STRATEGIES

1: INTRODUCTION: THE CHANGING MARKET FOR TALENT   3
When Talent Was King
HR's Strategic Opportunities
Opportunities Ahead
Plan of the Book
Why Talent?

2: "GETTING" BUSINESS STRATEGY   27
Business Strategy Barriers
The Role and Scope of Business Strategies
Business Strategy Models
New Business Strategy Landscape

3: VALUING TALENT   58
Working For/Belonging To
The History of Talent
Valuing Talent: Four Realities

PART II BUILDING, DELIVERING, AND MEASURING TALENT STRATEGIES

4: TALENT STRATEGIES: SCANNING   87
Talent Strategies Management Cycle
Business Strategies

5: TALENT STRATEGY BUILDING   114
      Talent Strategy Components

6: TALENT FLOW STRATEGIES   142
      Signature Talent Strategy Successes
      Talent Flow

7: TALENT ENGAGEMENT STRATEGIES   182
      More Than ''Being There''
      Talent Engagement Processes

8: MEASURING AND IMPROVING TALENT STRATEGIES   208
      Measuring Value Creation
      Measurement Perspectives: Types, Stages, and Balanced Measures
      Talent Process Measures

     Epilogue: Who Owns Talent Strategies?   233
      The Case for HR

     Index   241

Talent Strategies Are

Business Strategies

CHAPTER 1

◪ INTRODUCTION: THE CHANGING MARKET FOR TALENT

WHEN SPEAKING TO AN ANNUAL conference of human resources professionals in 2000, Gary Hamel—consultant, academic, and author of *Competing for the Future*—disparaged the clichéd claims of most if not all companies that "people are our most important asset." Instead, Hamel asserted unequivocally to his audience, "People are *all* there is to an organization." Although Hamel may have been preaching to the choir considering the setting, few business leaders or human resources (HR) practitioners—and especially recruiting professionals— would have challenged this claim during the past five years. Or rather, they wouldn't have done so until the NASDAQ and dot-com busts of mid-2000; the technology, telecommunications, and overall employment swoons that soon followed; and the economy-wide disruption touched off by the September 11, 2001, terrorist attacks on the United States.

When talent was king

From the mid- to late 1990s talent was king. In 1999, for example, when the Information Technology Association of America (ITAA), an Arlington, Virginia–based industry association, polled its eleven thousand information technology (IT) member companies to get a sense of their hiring needs for 2000, some astounding numbers came back. For a national IT workforce base of 10.4 million, ITAA member companies projected needs for an additional 1.6 million workers. And, apprehensively, they expected that nine hundred thousand of these positions would go begging because of a lack of sufficiently skilled applicants.

In other words, in one year the IT workforce—or at least a big approximation of it—could swell an additional 15 percent, yet end up nearly a million workers shy of its collective employment plans.[1] And these were not McJobs—poorly paid positions with no career future. These were high-paying, skill-rich, benefit-wielding career opportunities.[2]

These numbers got a lot of press and the ITAA members' cumulative workforce plight became a sort of recruiting poster for what had come to be termed the War for Talent:[3] the struggles of employers to land "up skill" employees in a cutthroat free-agent employment market. Suddenly and pervasively, tremendous business and revenue opportunities seemed to be hostage to a huge talent gap.

Of course, although the business information technology industry most visibly quantified the dilemma of recruitment and employment in the late 1990s, its story was hardly the only one told. Publications and news sources as varied as *Fortune,*[4] *Law Practice Management,*[5] *Investor's Business Daily,*[6] The North Carolina State Government News Service,[7] and the *Colorado Springs Independent*[8] headlined stories about crises in recruiting, paying, and keeping MBA graduates, college professors, lawyers, business consultants, drug research scientists, public school teachers, and even landscaping professionals.

Across a wide swath of industries and professions talent seemed to have all the cards. The unifying theme in all these different circumstances seemed to be the direct link between getting (and keeping) people and business success—and conversely, the threat to business if the right people could not be landed (or left the company). Trying to find, hire, and keep key talent was everybody's business, especially for HR. It was at least temporarily self-evident that talent was primarily an asset, not a cost.

But then, late in 2000, business conditions changed, and as quickly and dramatically as the IT talent shortage came, it seemed to evaporate. The Y2K crisis had come and gone. The lights went out for good at many dot-coms. In this technology employment-rich business segment, 139,643 employees at 927 companies were pink-slipped by summer's end in 2001.[9] In the broader technology business sector, legions of formerly successful high-tech companies watched their value-added products and services become margin-busting market commodities. And with this cumulative change in economic climate came radical downward adjustments to IT employment demand. The 2000 ITAA study, which was not released until April 2001, showed demand plunging 44 percent to 900,000 workers. Projected hiring shortfalls plunged even faster, down 53 percent to 425,000. All this occurred, of course, before the steamroller effects of 2001's economy-wide disruptions and layoffs.

And these effects, once they came were enough to make your head spin. It was as if the help-wanted pages—and the business pages—had turned into the obituary pages. In the first half of 2001, U.S. companies outlined plans to eliminate some 777,362 jobs, compared with 613,960 in all of 2000.[10] And it proved to be only the opening act to the cuts and threats of cuts that followed. Since the tragedies of September 11, 2001, companies—predominantly in telecommunications, but also in computers, electronics, industrial goods, and transportation—made a total of 624,411 additional job cuts. This roughly three-month total exceeded the twelve-month totals from each year from 1993 through 1997.[11] November jobs cuts were 181,412, more than quadrupling the 44,152 cuts of November 2000. Even though, as it turns out, simultaneous waves of hiring and layoffs have been coexisting for years—in good economic times and bad—these were nevertheless sobering workforce reversals. Did they signal that all the importance attached to talent in U.S. industry had been a mirage all along?

In the rubble of many workplaces, where hiring had been replaced by layoffs and signing bonuses by severance packages, business leaders responsible for human capital issues understandably scrambled to get their bearings. Having experienced a frenetic upward market where they often could not keep pace, they were suddenly just as apt to be in as deep a downward cycle—and probably with some of their own employment concerns—trying to make sense. Talent issues imploded, moving from the top of the agenda to the bottom. What is next?

HR's strategic opportunities

The objective of *Successful Talent Strategies* is to make both a case and a blueprint for developing talent strategies in a dynamic and market-intensive economy where acquiring, deploying, and preserving human capital—talent that matters—defines competitive advantage and success for many enterprises. Although we believe that the logical advocates, agents, and orchestrators for talent strategies are business HR leaders and teams, we'll strike an early note of caution: HR leaders have most often come up short in positioning or preparing themselves to devise, communicate, and execute market-responsive talent strategies aligned in meaningful ways with business strategies. Although few may doubt HR's strategic aspirations, many—including many in HR—question their strategic capabilities and stature.

For example, according to the results of a recent survey conducted jointly by the Society for Human Resource Management (SHRM) and The Ohio State University's Fisher College of Business, HR profession-als—by their own admission—fall well short of being fully integrated strategic partners (see Exhibit 1-1). If, even in the midst of the recent talent wars, HR did not achieve strategic stature, when will it have another chance?

Perhaps that chance will come soon. It still seems somewhat risky to predict the imminent reemergence of talent and skill shortages. Yet, at the same time, there seems to be little doubt that three fundamental factors—population, workforce composition, and employment marketplace dynamics—point in that direction.

"Baked in" shortages

The first of these fundamental factors is population: America's baby boomers are already swelling the ranks of the AARP.[12] Current layoffs, downsizings, and economic distress do not change the fact that for every individual joining the workforce in the United States, an individual-and-a-half (and trending toward two) is leaving. The number of people entering the U.S. workforce is declining and won't start increasing until 2018, when the echo boomers, who are now entering elementary school, begin working. Even at that juncture, the fastest growing population age segment will be people fifty-five years and older. Add to this the first blip in a possibly new trend in U.S. workforce demographics: the proportion of mothers opting to participate in the workforce may have peaked, and may be declining. In 2000, according to the U.S. Census Bureau, 55 percent of mothers with children under one year of age were working or looking for work. That is down from 1998, when the labor

Exhibit 1-1. HR's evaluation of its strategic role.

"In your opinion, what best describes the role of human resources in your organization?"	*Self-evaluation (n = 539)*
Fully integrated partner	24%
Primarily reactive to organizational needs	25%
Partially integrated strategic partner	48%

Based on information from SHRM®/Fisher College HR Strategies, Stages of Development and Organization Size Survey.

force participation rate for this group was almost 60 percent, and shows the first decrease since at least 1976.

Meanwhile, on the demand side, December 2001 data from the Bureau of Labor Statistics (BLS) show at least 58 million job openings available by 2010 for a labor force that will fall more than 5 million workers short of meeting these needs. In the interval, 22 million new jobs will be created and 36 million more openings will result from retirements. More than 90 percent of the new job growth will be in the service sector (see Exhibit 1-2), and the greatest growth—at 7 million jobs—will occur in professional specialty occupations (see Exhibit 1-3). A total of 12 million jobs, combining the 7 million professional specialty jobs and 5 million service jobs, will need to be filled by college or vocational program graduates. But here we face a shortfall approaching 3.5 million workers—workers who will need postsecondary education and skills.

And lest we think that the difference can be made up by immigration, the same circumstances—only worse—apply in other industrialized nations. The top fifty industrialized countries are either at, or

Exhibit 1-2. Employment by major industry division, 1990, 2000, and projected 2010.

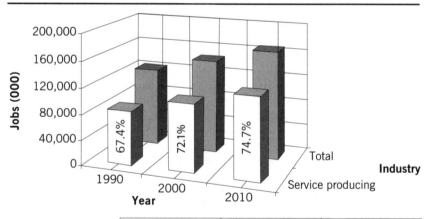

	1990	2000	2010
□ Service producing	83,854	104,930	125,390
▣ Total	124,324	145,594	167,754

Exhibit 1-3. Percentage employment increase by occupation 2000–2010.

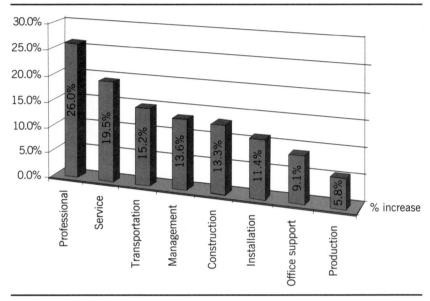

Based on information from BLS 2000 to 2010 American workforce projections by occupation.

below, zero population growth. Japan's population is shrinking, as is that of each of the countries in southern Europe—Portugal, Spain, Italy, and Greece. By the end of this new millennium Italy's population, which is now 60 million, could contract to about 20 million. And Japan's population, currently at 125 million, could be down to between 50 and 55 million. On both a national and international scale, talent scarcity is baked in. The developed world simply has a diminishing number of experienced managerial and technical workers in the working prime of life—on the talent side, the future is about accomplishing more with less.

Talent-intensive productivity

This brings us to the second fundamental factor, which concerns the level of talent needed now and in the future. With the zero-sum population trends pointing to a future need for higher-order, brains-over-bodies talent, there is already indisputable evidence that an increasing number of businesses are talent-intensive in the share of intellectual, skill, and customer relationship content of the products and services they deliver. Various studies show, for example, that up to 85 percent of a corporation's value is already based on these intangible assets.[13] According to a recent *Business Week* estimate, employment costs now absorb almost 87 percent of the output of nonfinancial corporations.[14] In today's knowledge-, service-, and brand-intensive economy, more value is added at the beginning of the product or service value chain (in research and innovation) and at the end (in customization and service) than in the middle (manufacturing and distribution).

Business value has been trending toward intangibles for some time now. For example, fifty years ago, tangible assets such as real estate, equipment, and inventories represented 78 percent of the assets of U.S. nonfinancial corporations. Today, the proportion is 53 percent, according to Federal Reserve data.[15] Even in manufacturing, the units of raw materials (since 1945), energy (since 1950), and physical labor (since 1900) needed for an additional unit of output have steadily *decreased* at a compound rate of about 1 percent. Yet, at the same time (though beginning much earlier, in 1880), the amount of information and knowledge needed for that same unit of output have *increased* at a compound rate of 1 percent. (See Exhibit 1-4.)

If this is true even in the steadily shrinking manufacturing segment, what does it suggest for other parts of the economy? Some management experts argue that the asset value of many businesses—the difference between their market and book values—actually reflects so-called people-embodied skills.[16] Looked at this way, intangibles that go by names such as *goodwill* and *brand leadership* more accurately reflect market and investor confidence in the difference-making capabilities of the businesses' talent.

A large segment of this talent consists of the much-heralded population of knowledge workers. In 1999 management authority Peter Drucker estimated that knowledge workers already comprised two-fifths of the U.S. workforce.[17] To this is added a smaller but faster grow-

Exhibit 1-4. Trend towards intangibles in production.

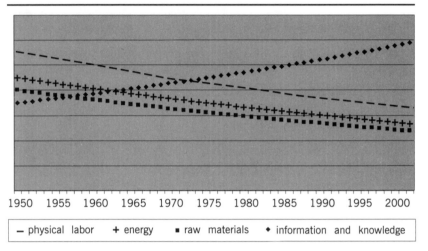

| 1950 | 1955 | 1960 | 1965 | 1970 | 1975 | 1980 | 1985 | 1990 | 1995 | 2000 |

— physical labor   + energy   ▪ raw materials   ♦ information and knowledge

ing segment doing both knowledge work *and* manual work, what Drucker terms *technologists*.[18]

People who perform this knowledge-intensive work ultimately have a unique value. Knowledge-intensive workers actually own—stored and whirring between their ears—the means of their production. It is a portable means of production, and because of this portability, organizations ultimately need talent more than talent needs organizations.[19] Nobel Laureate and University of Chicago economist Gary Becker estimates that per person, human capital wealth ranges from $500,000 to $5 million, depending on age, education, nature of work, and other factors. This translates to a value of as much as $180 trillion in the United States alone, according to data from Knowledge Universe, roughly 78 percent of U.S. combined financial, social, human capital, and other assets.

Having a workforce that is accessible, skilled, motivated, and efficiently deployed is now—and increasingly will be—a key differentiator of business performance and financial success. (In Chapter 2 we will see this is especially true as businesses, shaking off the vestiges of the New Economy get back down to strategy business, this time focused on customer-based strategies.) And if getting that workforce is a demographic challenge, it is also a competitive challenge in a revolutionized—some would say radicalized—employment marketplace.

The employment marketplace

The third fundamental factor is the emergence of this noisy, bustling, transaction-intensive, competitive, and disorderly external marketplace for skills and employment. This was the field of competition during the most recent talent wars.

While business organizations nearly always experience the disruptive intrusion of unpredictable, unforgiving market forces and demands on their products, structures, operations, and most carefully reasoned plans, disruptive market forces have only recently emerged for recruiting and employment.

This market is essentially employer-created and its current dynamics are relatively new—only about twenty years old. Its origins are in the market-induced, nearly simultaneous, and economy-wide employer decisions to abandon a formerly stable employer/employee social contract, replacing long-term employment with employment that is tenuous, contingent, and short lived. During the last five to ten years, market noise and activity have expanded exponentially because of the spread of the online information exchange capacities of e-mail and the Internet. As we see in Exhibit 1-5, employers of all sizes routinely access the market for their talent needs, often in preference to internal promotion.

As the economy surged and workers basked in a seller's market, it often proved difficult to compete for the specific (and attractively priced) blend of talent needed to exploit hot but fleeting business opportunities. And even for those businesses competing successfully in acquiring talent, the battle had only begun because many workers, even when newly employed, continued to test the market. That the market has turned for now to the buyer's advantage does not make it any less a market—and the trends in population and workforce-skill needs point to it heating up again.

Exhibit 1-5. Percentage who agree: "Most employees are hired from outside the organization."

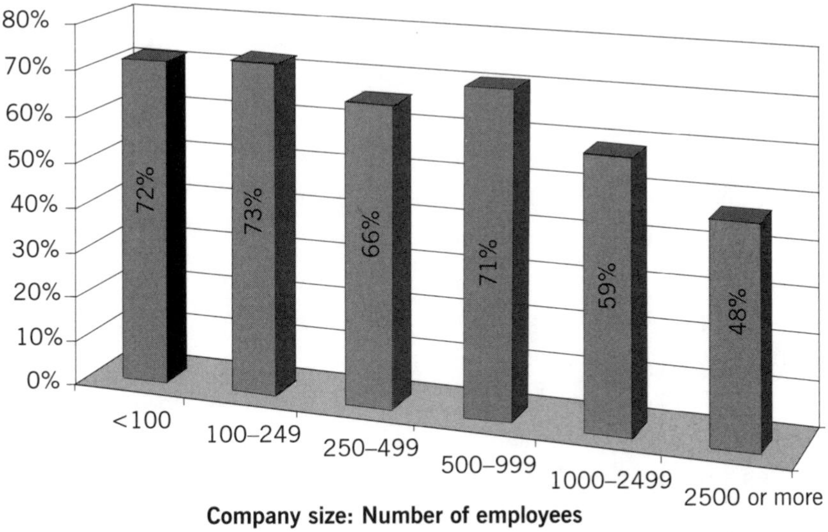

Company size: Number of employees

Bar chart values by company size:
- <100: 72%
- 100–249: 73%
- 250–499: 66%
- 500–999: 71%
- 1000–2499: 59%
- 2500 or more: 48%

Based on information from SHRM®/Fisher College HR Strategies, Stages of Development and Organization Size Survey.

Opportunities ahead

Because of these three fundamental trends, there is, more than ever, the need for businesses to be purposefully strategic about their access to talent. The need will be even more urgent if companies do not understand the reality. In its ongoing research about the war for talent, management-consulting firm McKinsey & Company found, in a 2000 study of sixty-nine hundred managers, that only 26 percent strongly agreed that talent was a top priority for their companies.[20] The reality is that talent in many organizations is an intermittent priority, with responsibilities dispersed throughout the organization and usually without a cohesive and coherent strategic view.

To address this need, there are opportunities ahead for HR to demonstrate its strategic capabilities. But if, to quote Shakespeare, the past is prologue, and HR's strategic achievements during the most recent talent wars are predictive of what lies ahead, those opportunities could again be wasted.

At the height of the talent wars, HR professionals succeeded in getting the attention of C-level executives who saw their business plans frustrated, delayed, or doomed by the challenge of acquiring the essential talent to fulfill them. But many simply did not deliver on the strategic opportunities and intentions they had. Instead, many got caught up in the short-term, tactical, and reactive; in setting higher priorities for *how* things should be accomplished over *what* should be accomplished; in making unrealistic projections of talent needs or talent availability (for example, the roll-up estimates of ITAA-member companies); in making single-factor instead of multifactor decisions; in taking flawed measures to reach flawed conclusions; in flailing around in activities that were out of step with the fundamentals of their businesses.

As a result, many HR professionals who found themselves frazzled but energized during the upside of the talent wars now find themselves returning with frustration and resignation to the usual abuse of the downside of today's talent massacres.

Executives and line managers question HR's contributions and capacity during times of business success—especially when it proves to be immensely difficult to find and keep much-needed talent. (I recall asking a senior sales executive what value HR expertise added to his screening and selection process. After reflecting for a moment, he responded: "About two weeks.") And during the tough times, such as those to which we've abruptly returned, they quickly challenge HR to defend its business value beyond doing the administrative dirty work of showing former employees the door. If talent is such a potent driver, and if HR is in the talent business yet still lacks strategic credibility, what can HR leaders do to establish, raise, or repair their credibility? How can they be more purposeful—and successful—in determining and delivering strategic value? We suggest that the best opportunity is now.

When McKinsey asked corporate officers in its 2000 survey whether HR should be a "high-impact partner to line managers in strengthening the talent pool," 88 percent of respondents reported that such a role was important or crucial. Yet, when asked if HR currently fulfills such a role, only 12 percent agreed.[21] If HR's strategy stock is low in a battered market, then this most dismal time may be among the very best for gearing up toward a strategic future.

Talent flow, talent engagement

Business enterprises have always been shaped by the realities of outside markets for products and services. But successful businesses do more than merely react to or cope with market forces. In one way or another—formally or informally, concisely or elaborately, systematically or intuitively—their leaders step above the competitive battles to plan: that is, to identify, exploit, and sustain market advantage through business strategies and strategy initiatives.

For HR leaders to effectively contribute to the success of business strategies, especially in talent-intensive business environments in the years ahead, HR leaders must similarly identify, exploit, and sustain competitive advantage—in this case through talent that is available, equipped, informed, and fully engaged.

This goes beyond administrative care and feeding. It also goes beyond mimicking what others are doing if there is not a fit with strategy. To effectively support business strategies, I believe it to be essential that HR must also conceive, fashion, and successfully champion explicit strategies for:

- Ensuring access to sufficient *talent flow*—people at the right time (though not for all time, or even a substantial portion of their careers); in the right numbers; with the right mix of skills and capabilities; under the right terms of employment
- Actively *engaging* (rather than passively employing) that talent in ways that support and achieve business strategy objectives

But toughest and most important of all, HR—or whoever is ultimately responsible for the talent flow and engagement processes we will discuss—must do it in terms that best fit the strategy and resources of the business. *They must understand, establish, and exploit links between the value that customers derive from an organization's products and services and the things that talented people can do to create and enhance that value.* Business strategies and talent strategies may be impressive but empty vehicles if they do not establish the connection between what customers want and what people do. This is an obvious relationship, especially for business leaders or anyone in a one-to-one business-to-customer relationship. But it is also easy to lose track of this relationship—or to become confused about it—as organizations grow and as people's work efforts become increasingly indirect.

HR shapes, sizes, and roles—and strategy opportunities

The strategy perspectives and approaches we'll be considering tend to be shaped, sized, and designed for the structure and cultures of the organizations in which they operate. Different structures create different strategy opportunities and face different drawbacks.

For example, the leader of a centralized, corporate, multifunction HR shared services department in a *Fortune* 500 business is more likely to devote at least some undivided time to business strategy issues and the implications of those issues for talent priorities and programs. The results are often—although by no means always—talent strategies formulated over months and executed over years backed by board level approval and sizable resources in HR infrastructure, expertise, internal staff, and external consulting assistance. These talent strategies are likely to align with long-term corporate business strategy, yet they may become incoherent as responsibilities and accountabilities are dispersed through organization layers or lose strength by the time they reach the remote outposts of the business. As a result, these strategies can actually end up having little day-to-day impact at the business unit level. (One HR executive we talked to contrasted the difference between her earlier employment as an HR manager in corporate HR at a *Fortune* 500 property and casualty insurance firm with her subsequent experience at a start-up media company, by commenting: "At 'P & C, Inc.' you could almost feel the impact and meaning of strategy losing steam as it moved down from the executive offices and out to the perimeters of the business. At 'Start-up Media' everybody seemed to be directly connected to the strategy. Nobody could claim not to know what we were trying to achieve.'')

In medium-size businesses, or in the self-contained strategic business units (SBUs) into which many large corporations have been parceled since the 1970s, business and talent strategies face different constraints and opportunities. Here the view of overall business strategy is more apt to get obscured, while SBU strategies—business and talent—are clear, especially if the HR leader or professional succeeds in partnering with a strategically minded SBU head who knows the value of his or her talent resources. Strategy execution time frames may be shorter—usually one to two years—and resources will be scarcer, but there is some room to think and act for the long term.

The real strategy opportunities and constraints belong to HR professionals who are in stand-alone roles in smaller organizations; or who deal with the volatile upsides and downsides of emerging technology businesses; or who must be both strategists and hands-on practitioners in smaller companies (the majority of U.S. business establishments currently have fewer than twenty-five employees). They may well wonder—if, indeed, there is a spare moment for it to occur to them—how the more deliberative HR strategies of a huge corporation scale to their practical needs and short-fused deliverables. Yet leaders in small businesses expect HR to be both quick and strategic (that is, know the business) about the acquisition and deployment of people resources. These leaders value HR as a value-added discipline not as a separate department function. These HR professionals also are apt to be less insulated than their large corporation counterparts from the upheavals in the marketplace for products, services, and talent.

But at the same time, these HR professionals also can have a larger window of strategic opportunity. (As did the HR leader quoted earlier). She typically has direct access to C-level executives—and certainly C-level executives have direct access to her. She can be more nimble with employment initiatives that have real line of sight to the bottom line.

Shouldered with multiple HR functions (processes, really), she also has the opportunity to integrate, reinforce, and establish consistency among those processes. In short, she can have an impact on talent strategies at a juncture where succeeding with business strategy has the biggest payoff—or consequence—for business survival and growth.

Older business and employment relationships once gave real advantage to large, integrated companies in stable markets with long planning horizons, while constraining aspiring start-up companies. That advantage has often shifted dramatically with the rise in competitive markets—at least to the extent that nimble and focused business can take advantage of those markets.

The bottom line is that HR strategies, or what we will term *talent strategies*, are not only for the large, resource-rich brand name. Indeed, talent strategies we will describe here are equally viable in decentralized SBUs and in small- to medium-size business organizations.

Market-facing talent strategies

It is important that talent strategies, in the vernacular of business strategy, be market-facing. In *HR Scorecard* Brian Becker, Mark Huselid, and Dave Ulrich stress the importance of HR strategy alignment being in synch both *horizontally* (across internal HR functions such as recruiting, compensation, benefits, development—all of which bear on talent) and *vertically* with business strategy.[22] We focus here as well on another type of alignment—*externally* between talent strategy and the realities of the employment market.

It is a tricky business. HR must act in concert with business strategies in the company's product/service markets while sometimes contending with differing, even counter cyclical circumstances in the markets where it competes for talent. (The clearest example, of course, is that when a business is most successful it becomes hardest to find and keep key talent.) The point is that the forces of business marketplace, business strategies, talent strategies, and talent employment marketplace are unmistakably interrelated and dynamic.

Although the usual top-down strategic sequence is for product and service markets to influence business strategies and business strategies in turn to drive talent strategies, it is conceivable that employment markets may directly drive business strategy. For example, at the height of the technology talent wars, at least one Silicon Valley–based optical networking company moved all of its operations to New Jersey in the interest of sourcing and hiring Lucent and AT&T technologists. Conversely, a business might sink if it is unable to quickly streamline or dismantle an outmoded or bloated employment infrastructure.

Whatever the scenario, in order to succeed, the players (including HR) in this market system must understand that all the components and the system itself are in constant motion. (See Exhibit 1-6.) Favorable or unfavorable, product and service markets do not stand still and neither do employment markets. The trick for all players, including HR, is to be strategic, coordinated, practical, and nimble. In short, talent strategies are market strategies. To be effective, it is essential that they be thought through and crafted with the same planning, clear-headedness, and commitment that go into successful business strategies.

Plan of the book

The eight chapters of *Successful Talent Strategies* are organized in two parts. Part I, which includes Chapter 1, Chapter 2, and Chapter 3, is a primer on business strategies and talent.

Every business has strategies—by intent or by default—for how it intends to compete, survive, and succeed in its markets and industry. But what are strategies exactly? Are they plans? Are they actions? Are they both? How are plans thought through, developed, communicated, or acted on? And most fundamental: *How do business strategies create value for customers, and in what tangible way does talent contribute to that value?*

Business strategies—and talent strategies as well—are flavored by the business environment and business thinking of the times in which they are hatched. As we'll see in Chapter 2, one era's business strategy

Exhibit 1-6. System of strategies and markets.

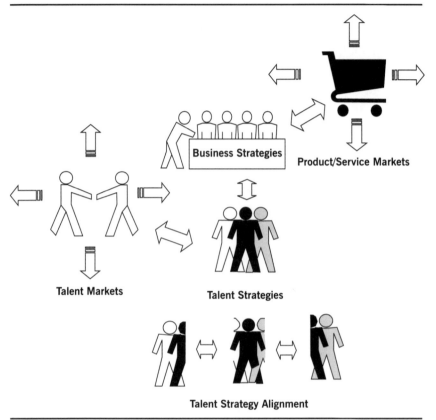

breakthroughs are another era's poor fits, if not heresies. It is important to pinpoint the essentials of a model for building and delivering talent strategies.

Chapter 3 complements Chapter 2's strategy essentials with talent essentials, a primer on when, how, and why talent has positioned itself as a leveraging force in today's business world.

Part I, in summation, has three objectives:

1. To track the relationships among business events, business strategies, and the role of human capital in those strategies
2. To provide basic working definitions, parameters, and exam-

ples—including some of the things that strategies are *not*—to underpin what follows

3. To show how strategies have evolved to a point where talent is indeed the preeminent resource in strategies driven by customers and in relationships with customers

In Part II, we shift attention to the process of designing, building, delivering, measuring, and improving talent strategies. The orientation here is around building a strategy framework to prioritize and deliver changes that fit with business strategies. Chapter 4 covers essential strategy groundwork:

- Scanning and evaluating the internal environment of business strategies, business structure, talent processes, and existing talent resources to create a baseline for talent strategy direction
- Scanning and evaluating the external marketplace of talent and competing employment alternatives

The path to strategic credibility is not through complaint or gimmickry, but rather through some not-so-surprising fundamentals. These include understanding what drives business value, synching up your efforts with those drivers; delivering flawless transactions, and, finally, raising the bar beyond transactions to processes.

Sound, competitive talent strategies forge the essential links between what a business is trying to achieve through strategy and what it can deliver via its people resources. Talent strategies are business-wide strategies, not merely HR strategies. Talent strategies help to differentiate businesses in the markets where they compete for customers. They also help to differentiate businesses in the markets where they compete for talent.

Chapters 5 to 8 detail the process of strategy building (Chapter 5), strategy delivery (Chapters 6 and 7), and strategy measurement/improvement (Chapter 8), using as a focus two fundamental types of business-wide talent strategy processes:

1. Talent flow includes strategy initiatives to source, recruit, hire (in the broadest sense), deploy, and retain talent. Talent flow strategies also include what have become or are becoming crucial talent relationship activities that blend into active recruiting before employment and may continue as ongoing contact after employment. Talent flow involves establishing and managing enduring relationships.

2. Talent engagement includes strategy initiatives designed to maximize the value of the employment exchange under new traditions and new models of work and employment.

Talent flow strategies and talent engagement strategies are not mutually exclusive. They overlap rather than abut each other. They influence each other; indeed, one criteria for selecting or building successful talent strategy initiatives is that they do double, even triple duty. They represent useful ways of thinking about talent issues in process terms as well as allocating resources.

The purpose here is not to reinvent HR organization structure. The idea, however, is to focus away from bottom-up reactionary, purely administrative, transactional, and too-often lightly regarded functions and focus toward transformational process-based strategies. Neatly or jealously demarcated so-called silo functions such as recruiting, compensation, training, and systems—whether realized in formally distinct functions, as in large corporations, or in mind-set as in smaller businesses—can be deadly; HR professionals need to cross boundaries in the interests of delivering strategic talent solutions.

Chapter 8 deals with crucial issues of measuring and improving talent strategies—measures based on cost, measures based on operations, and balanced measures. Measures need to be of a piece with talent strategies: The ideal is to measure talent efforts and outcomes that have the most significance for customer-perceived value. The ideal is to use these measures toward incremental, or if necessary, radical improvements in strategies and processes. One of the things that makes any business strategy easy to imagine but hard to realize is the failure to conceive and take measures that form the basis for improvement. Measurement is foresight rather than afterthought.

The idea for *Successful Talent Strategies* originated in what was a talent seller's marketplace. Currently, that market seems to belong to buyers—at least the few that are active in what has become an unforgiving, cut-rate market. However, neither circumstance makes it any less a marketplace. Whether in good times or in bad times, and whether there is a shortage or a surplus of people, businesses continue to have an appetite for skilled talent. Even in the distressful days of late October 2001, and in an industry setting as challenged as manufacturing, 80 percent of managers participating in a trade survey responded that their greatest challenge continued to be finding skilled talent.

As this book goes to press, it is difficult to predict whether "talent wars" or "talent massacres"—or something in-between—will be the essential feature of the employment landscape. Indications are emerging that recent economic, employment, and talent downturns may be brief. Among other things, the depth of the plunge may have been overstated. For example, Department of Labor monthly unemployment data show the unemployment rate for college-educated workers never climbed higher than 3.1 percent, reaching that level during December 2001. In February 2002, it was already down to 2.9 percent.

The much emphasized dot-com implosion turns out to have shuttered at most 10 percent of the seven thousand to ten thousand substantial, venture-funded Internet companies.[23] During the 2001 economic downturn, U.S. (talent-driven) productivity growth was 1.9 percent, well above the U.S. norm for the period 1973 to 1995, and nearly matching 1995 to 2000 productivity growth.

And at ground level, talent demand seems to be revving up. As one example, Dice Inc., an online recruiting service for technology professionals, listed about forty-six hundred job openings for the New York metro area at the end of February. While this represented a significant decrease from the ten thousand positions listed a year before, it is still a 15 percent increase from the end of December.

In the face of these certain demographically induced sourcing challenges, and with the realization of how talent intensive most businesses are, it seems amazing that relatively few businesses actually deal with people as a core resource deserving a strategic approach. Part of the reason may be that strategy building often seems to be a difficult, time-consuming, and even irrelevant concept—something that business competitive pressures do not allow for.

Our premise here is that systematic talent strategies can be practical and meaningful, and can have a real impact on people-intensive enterprises. Moreover, without business strategies, without an understanding of how that strategy translates into action, and, finally, without a strategic approach to people issues, business becomes an unacceptable combination of purposeless tactics and pure chance.

Why talent?

A word here about why we use the term *talent strategies* instead of, say, HR strategies or recruiting strategies. There are two reasons. First *Successful Talent Strategies* is about business-wide strategies, not departmental agendas. HR will succeed at a strategic level only if it succeeds in orchestrating and working across boundaries—including the boundaries of HR—and performing a discipline instead of being a function.

Second, we hope that talent conveys the nature of the human capital resources it represents. The word *talent* has ancient origins: originally as a unit of weight, then as a unit of monetary value, and then as a symbol for people's innate achievements.[24] Talent is more than an organization's conclave of employees:

- Talent represents employee skills and capabilities.
- Talent often assumes managerial talents, but it increasingly extends to a wider range of specialized organizational players.
- Talent represents the skills and capabilities of people hovering at shifting boundaries of organizations: for example, potential employees and contingent or contract workers.

- Talent may even include the skills and capabilities of people in other organizations—people nominally working on the other side of organization boundaries that future business needs may require crossing in order to form extended enterprises.

Notes

1. This IT workforce estimate roughly doubles the U.S. Department of Commerce estimate that the IT-producing industries employed roughly 5.6 million workers in 2000. Using that figure as a base, the ITAA member companies projected employment needs would represent an astounding 30 percent of the national IT workforce.

2. In 2000 (the last year for which data is available) the national average IT worker salary was $73,800, roughly twice the nation's average private-sector pay of $35,000 (up from a 1994 premium of 67 percent).

3. Origin of the term is credited to a series of survey studies conducted by management consulting firm McKinsey and Company beginning in 1997.

4. David Leonard, "The Talent Chase," *Fortune*, May 2000, p. 89.

5. "The Recruiting Wars: Profits vs. Inflated Salaries," *Law Practice Management*, April 1999.

6. "The Industry's Recruiting Wars Show No Signs of Easing," *Investor's Business Daily*, November 27, 2000.

7. "Recruiting Wars: School Recruiters in the Triangle Say the Wake County School System Is Going After Teachers Who Are Under Contract to Other Systems," *The Insider: North Carolina State Government News Service*, August 24, 1999.

8. "Responding to an Anticipated Shortage of 1,000 K-12 Teachers in Colorado Springs Next Fall, Local Superintendents and Principals Are Gearing Up for a Major Recruiting War," *Colorado Springs Independent*, February 22, 2001.

9. The Layoff Tracker is a list of layoffs at dot-com companies compiled since December 1999 by TheStandard.com, the online version of *The Industry Standard*. The list includes confirmed reports of staff reductions affecting ten or more workers at Internet-related companies, or from the Internet divisions of

offline firms. U.S. and foreign companies are included, but smaller companies are typically not included. This data is as of August 19, 2001.

10. Louis Uchitelle, "As Job Cuts Spread, Tears Replace Anger," *The New York Times*, August 5, 2001.

11. According to a survey conducted by Challenger, Gray & Christmas, the Chicago-based outplacement firm.

12. Thomas A. Stewart, "Dispatches from the Talent Wars" *Business 2.0*, May 23, 2001.

13. Brian E. Becker, Mark A. Huselid, and David Ulrich, *The HR Scorecard: Linking People, Strategy, and Performance* (Boston: Harvard Business School Press, 2001), p. IX.

14. Michael J. Mandel, "Restating the 90s," *BusinessWeek*, April 1, 2002, p. 52.

15. Greg Ip, "The Rise and Fall of Intangible Assets Leads to Shorter Company Life Spans," *The Wall Street Journal*, April 4, 2002, p. 1.

16. Gary Hamel and C.K. Prahalad, *Competing for the Future* (Boston: Harvard Business School Press, 1994), p. 255.

17. Peter F. Drucker, *Management Challenges for the 21st Century* (New York: HarperBusiness, 1999), p. 141.

18. Ibid., p. 149.

19. Ibid., p. 149.

20. Ed Michaels, Helen Handfield-Jones, and Beth Axelrod, *The War for Talent* (Boston: Harvard Business School Press, 2001), p. 158.

21. Ibid., p. 32.

22. Brian E. Becker, Mark A. Huselid, and Dave Ulrich, *The HR Scorecard: Linking People, Strategy, and Performance* (Boston: Harvard Business School Press, 2001), p. 133.

23. U.S. Department of Commerce Economic and Statistics Administration, *Digital Economy*, February 2002, p. vii.

24. One Greek talent, circa 500 to 300 B.C., equaled 25,800 grams, or 829 troy ounces of silver; which at today's market prices for silver would be about $37,000.

CHAPTER 2

◨ "GETTING" BUSINESS STRATEGY

ALL BUSINESSES HAVE STRATEGIES: STRATEGIES for what they want to achieve and how they propose to realize those achievements. The strategies may be simple or complex, formal or informal. They may be rock steady or constantly changing. They may be strategies for the long term or strategies for special circumstances such as restructuring, mergers, acquisitions, new business ventures, or business expansions. They may be good strategies that are poorly understood or sluggishly implemented—or poor but triumphant strategies salvaged by extraordinary focus, understanding, communication, and execution.

The plans that encompass these strategies may be stated as one thing—and operated as another. Strategies may go unnamed or be called by an often-interchangeable lexicon of names, such as plans, strategies, visions, missions, goals, objectives, core competencies, or competitive advantages. Like the perspectives on the proverbial elephant, perspectives on business strategies depend on whom you ask—and how the elephant, not to mention the jungle, is behaving.

Business strategy barriers

"Getting" business strategy is the indisputable starting point for any meaningful contribution to strategic processes. The company's strategies should form the basis for talent strategies—and more often than ever, talent is itself a pivotal competitive differentiator in business strategies. But, for a number of reasons, pinning down business strategies may be no easy matter. Some of the common hurdles include:

* *Business leaders may not articulate their strategies well.* Companies whose leaders capture the unique, compelling message of their company's strategies and are skilled, consistent, and unwavering in communicating this message through structures, processes, and actions as well as words, clearly improve chances that their strategies will work. However, when leaders go "off message" by being bland, unconvincing, cryptic or silent, the damaging effects ripple throughout an organization, leaving what the strategies actually are and how to accomplish them open to speculation and interpretation.

* *Business strategies compete for success in time-sensitive markets.* Compared with business circumstances fifty, twenty, ten, or even five years ago, businesses, their strategies, and the objectives of those strategies often race frantically against obsolescence. Businesses unveil new technologies and introduce entirely new product/service categories at a blistering pace, while on a parallel track, the network of business relationships and business financing arrangements to support them have moved apace. For example, although it took facsimile technology twenty-two years to generate sales of 10 million units, it took VCRs nine

years, CD players seven, PCs six, and Internet browsers only ten months.[1] Moore's Law, the remarkably sturdy forecast first phrased in 1964 by the cofounder of Intel that the amount of information storable on a given amount of silicon would roughly double every twelve to eighteen months, continues to be emblematic of the blistering pace of business and its underlying strategies.

• *Business strategies grow ever more subtle.* We mentioned in Chapter 1 that as much as 85 percent of a business's value may be based on intangible assets and that, for nonfinancial corporations, intangible assets represent more than 50 percent of all assets. Intangibles elude neat classification. And, to make things more challenging, it is often the context and blending of these assets—for example a unique combination of branded products, a rigorously trained sales force, a proprietary customer relationship management system, a product support infrastructure, and a carefully nurtured company image—linked to strategies, rather than formal strategies by themselves, that make the difference. The strategies are more than the some of their parts; and these contexts and combinations are difficult to master.[2]

• *Business strategies may be fragmented.* In an effort to channel complexity, companies almost inevitably parcel out strategy responsibilities into separate functions and projects assigned to different places, departments (including, for example, HR), and people. Taken to decentralized extremes, the strategy fragments get detached and the overall strategies obscured. Under these cannot-see-the-forest-for-the-trees circumstances, business strategies can be difficult to get in focus—and, of course, to coordinate and execute.

• *Strategies morph quickly in unstable markets.* In the new economy companies such as Amazon, Yahoo!, and eBay have pursued exploratory and constantly evolving strategies that try to take advantage of unanticipated and fleeting opportunities. Yahoo began as a Web site catalog, became a content aggregator, and recently emerged as a media network—all in an incrementally opportunistic rather than in a formally strategic way. Some would argue that in the information and service economy strategies sprout, mature, and whither so quickly that trying to stay "on strategy" is at best a distracting, frustrating, and unprofitable exercise.

• *Executive teams may not reach consensus on what strategies are.* Because of complexity, dynamic changes in markets, and nagging differences in opinion, a clear and fully committed strategy model may not emerge. Executive teams are often stretched thin. Team members may not actually see each other often. When they convene to deliberate strategy, they are likely to do so in circumstances combining insufficient information, intervening distractions, and incomplete trust. One estimate is that fully three quarters of executive teams never reach full consensus on crucial strategic issues such as corporate image, intended relationships with customers, or even product and service attributes.[3] And when this happens:

• *Announced strategies may not always be real strategies.* Absent consensus, executive teams may hide their differences behind pretended solidarity and vague statements of strategic purpose. Such announced strategies may represent a company's effort to put a good face on the situation. They tend to be lofty, bland, and indistinguishable. Hard to find fault with, but also hard to do anything about.

• *Strategies may be "visions without decisions."* Strategies may be authentic but not backed up by resources. In uncertain environments business leaders may be particularly risk averse. Although leaders and teams might reach true consensus over a vision of future events and intentions, the vision may not be backed by commitment in resources, structures, systems, or processes. Is there a strategy in mind? Yes. Is there a strategy in action? No.

• *Words, ideas, and actions labeled* strategies *are not really strategies.* Consider the spectrum of actions and ideas that occur in organizations, all the way from the most mundane, repetitive tasks to the most visionary or abstract ideas. Business strategies may be confused with supporting processes (strategy planning, for example), management techniques (management by walking around, Total Quality Management, or process reengineering) or even big picture philosophy (vision statements). While business strategies may involve or benefit from some or all of these things, they are not strategies.

 • *''Getting'' business strategies demands proactive and rigorous understanding.* Those intent on ''getting'' business strategies or operating at the strategy level need to bring something to the table in preparation and understanding. Although all business strategies are, at least in some ways, unique, they also almost always bear the stamp of strategies that have been thought through and tried before. Learning something about these models is one important foundation for understanding real strategies.

The role and scope of business strategies

Our learning path begins with a few strategy definitions—a way of clarifying the role and scope. We'll then focus on seven strategy models, showing how each one reflects the economic and business conditions that influenced it. We'll then shift our attention to the context of today's business strategies.

Business strategy definitions

Settling on a single, concise definition for the role of business strategy is risky, in part because of the hundreds of theories, books, articles, consultants, and schools, devoted to the topic.[4] The eight definitions listed in Exhibit 2-1 give only a sample, but scanning them reveals some baseline elements, which include:

 • Business strategies are long-term tools.
 • Business strategies are both plans and actual patterns of behavior.
 • Business strategies combine intentions and adaptation to events.
 • Business strategies help to minimize business risks and maximize business achievements.
 • Business strategies translate ideas into accomplishments.

Exhibit 2-1. Business strategy definitions.

---

1. **Strategy is the match between what a company can do (because of its resources and organizational capabilities) within the universe of what it might do** (because of opportunities or competitive pressures).[1]
2. **Strategy is a long-term direction that says what you are trying to accomplish and how you are going to do it.** Strategy is concerned with developing long-term objectives, devising a coherent set of plans for achieving them, and then allocating the resources needed to carry out those plans.[2]
3. **Strategy is the creation of a unique and valuable position, involving a different set of activities.** The essence of strategic positioning is to choose activities that are different from rivals'.[3]
4. **Strategy answers two basic questions: Where do you want to go? And how do you want to get there?**[4]
5. **Strategy converts (the) Theory of the Business (a set of assumptions as to what its business is, what it objectives are, how it defines results, who its customers are, what the customers value and pay for) into performance.** Its purpose is to enable an organization to achieve its desired results in an unpredictable environment. Strategy allows an organization to be *purposefully opportunistic.*[5]
6. **Strategy formation achieves the essential fit between internal strengths and weaknesses and external threats and opportunities.**[6]
7. **The core of any business strategy is the customer value proposition, which describes the unique mix of product and service attributes, customer relations, and corporate image that a company offers.** It defines how the business will differentiate itself.[7]
8. **A business's strategy is its plan for developing and sustaining an advantage in the product/service marketplace(s) in which it competes.**[8]
9. **Organizations develop plans for the future and they also evolve patterns out of the past.** We can call one *intended* strategy and the other *realized* strategy.[9]
10. **What does strategy mean in the new economy? . . . a few key strategic processes . . . a handful of simple rules.**[10]

---

[1] Kenneth R. Andrews, *The Concept of Corporate Strategy* (New York: Richard D. Irwin, 1971).

[2] William C. Finnie, *Hands-On Strategy: The Guide to Crafting Your Company's Future* (New York: John Wiley & Sons, Inc., 1994), p. 5.

[3] Michael E. Porter, "What is Strategy?" *Harvard Business Review,* November–December, 1996, p. 68.

[4] "Making Strategy," *The Economist,* March 1, 1997.

[5] Peter F. Drucker, *Management Challenges for the 21st Century* (New York: HarperBusiness, 1999), p. 43.

[6] Henry Mintzberg and Joseph Lampel, "Reflecting on the Strategy Process," *Sloan Management Review,* Spring 1999, p. 22.

[7] Robert S. Kaplan and David P. Norton, "Having Trouble with Your Strategy? Map It," *Harvard Business Review,* September–October 2000, p. 172.

[8] Brian E. Becker, Mark A. Huselid, and David Ulrich, *The HR Scorecard: Linking People, Strategy, and Performance* (Boston: Harvard Business School Press, 2001), p. 2.

[9] Henry Mintzburg, *The Rise and Fall of Strategic Planning* (New York: The Free Press, 1994), p. 24.

[10] Kathleen M. Eisenhardt and Donald N. Sull, "Strategy As Simple Rules," *Harvard Business Review,* January 2001, p. 107.

- Business strategies integrate what is being accomplished (objectives) with how they're being accomplished (ideas, plans, resources, initiatives, and actions).
- Business strategies require resource choices.
- Business strategies require evaluation of internal strengths/weaknesses and external opportunities/risks.
- Business strategies focus on customers and what customers value.

Robert Grant, in his book *Contemporary Strategy Analysis,* presents a narrower list of what he considers to be three fundamental elements:

1. Long-term, simple objectives
2. Profound understanding of customers and competitors
3. Objective appraisal and use of resources[5]

Business strategy contexts

Business strategies also have contexts, frames of reference, and the level and point of view of the strategy makers. For example:

- Business strategies are developed at corporate and business-unit levels.
- Business strategies (corporate or business unit) may reflect head-to-head competition and the shaping of events and outcomes vis-à-vis the industry or specific competitors.
- Business strategies (corporate or business unit) may be adaptive, seeking a defensible place in a wider universe of an industry or niche within an industry. (See Exhibit 2-2.)

Business strategy models

Business strategy models—templates or abstracts of real business strategies—most often reflect the substantial impact of historic events and

Exhibit 2-2. Business strategy contexts.

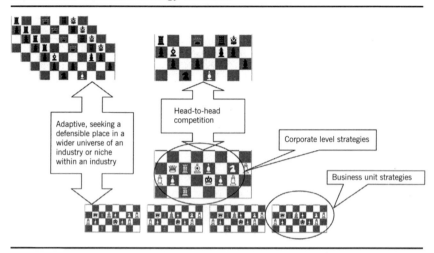

economic conditions on industries and businesses. One caution about these strategy models is that they are artifacts, somebody's—a business leader's, an academic's, or a consultant's—after-the-fact view of what happened. Henry Ford, whose thinking and actions figure prominently in early business strategies, once said: "History is more or less bunk."[6] More recently, when Louis V. Gerstner Jr. took the helm as chair and chief executive of IBM, he emphasized early on that, as far as Big Blue's strategy direction was concerned, "The last thing IBM needs now is a vision."[7] It is abundantly clear that companies and their leaders do not choose strategies like a suit off a rack or cereal off a grocery shelf or (with a nod to Henry Ford) cars off an assembly line.

This being said, the short history (it goes back roughly sixty years) of business strategy thinking is important for three reasons. First, understanding these models reduces a flood of strategy variations down to a manageable set.

Second, even the most disfavored strategy approaches continue to intrude on today's business behavior. Concepts like cash cow, diversification, and vertical integration become, and continue to be, part of business vocabulary. And despite warnings from academics and consultants about "getting stuck in the middle," businesses often pursue blended strategies, thereby building on, borrowing, or cobbling ideas and elements from different strategy models

Third, the cycle of these strategy models shows, as history often does, that seemingly new, even radical ideas, are not always entirely new. New strategies may be old strategy types reborn, refined, or repackaged. Understanding these models is good preparation for the present and future of business strategy.

This history is brief, not because business leaders suddenly invented strategy and started behaving strategically—after all, the term *strategy* comes from the ancient Greek word for "generalship"—but because business strategies were not systematically scrutinized and dissected, or at least not in the way that they have been practiced since the emergence of management science in the late 1940s and early 1950s. Since that time, business practices and strategies have been tracked exhaustively and translated into theories, models, and approaches aimed at repeating strategic successes or sidestepping strategic disasters. For our purposes we will describe each model in terms of its underlying concept. These concepts are useful shorthand—a way of capturing prevailing ways that businesses think, operate, and compete.

1. Integration strategies

Our first model represents the large, complex, and centralized business organizations that emerged during the first quarter of the century and grew through vertical integration—gaining control of materials and processes all the way from raw materials to customer. These businesses replaced what would now be described as virtual enterprises—loose business confederations orchestrated by entrepreneurs who contracted and subcontracted virtually all work.

These new configurations reflected three new business realities for their time:

1. Business owners, seeing a future of long-term sustained growth, did not want to be held hostage to the uncertainties of contracted resources—instead they wanted these resources (including peo-

ple) under their umbrella. And, not incidentally, they wanted to capture for themselves the profits previously earned by contractors and subcontractors.

2. The scale and complexity of new manufacturing and related processes could be better orchestrated under the same umbrella—often through the communication and coordination activities of a new class of employed supervisors, managers, and administrative personnel.

3. While the new technology was wondrous, it was also too large and expensive to be owned, operated, and housed by subcontractors with casual, transient workforces. Only large companies with deep pockets, adequate facilities, and access to a trained, captive workforce could expect to manage and profit from the expense.

Thus, early business strategies expressed themselves through these new vertically integrated business structures. The typical, and probably also the most prominent, example was Ford Motor Company, whose River Rouge industrial complex near Detroit literally transformed raw materials into finished automobiles.

Companies such as Ford managed growth and complexity through many-layered people organizations. Layered hierarchies became channels for communication, for decision gatekeeping, for indoctrination and supervision, and for experience building and backup. Slicing through those layers were functional organizations—finance, manufacturing, sales, marketing, law, administration, and eventually personnel administration—realms of specialized expertise, another way to tackle and conquer complexity.

However, by midcentury, with the centralized, convoluted hierarchies of companies like Ford, General Motors, DuPont, and Standard Oil groaning under their own weight, and with government regulation threatening to dismantle competition-stifling vertical business arrangements, many companies began reversing the cycle of centralization by creating decentralized divisions.

2. Planning strategies

A nearly coinciding phenomenon was the application of new quantitative management and analytic techniques originally developed by World War II Allied planners to contend with the massive human and logistics demands of a lengthy, global conflict. Postwar, these techniques quickly evolved into a new discipline dubbed *management science*. Management science was deployed to harness business systems and operations whose complexity and breadth had outmatched prewar methods—and whose complexity and breadth only increased in the postwar years.

Management science emphasized budgeting and cost control—doing things by the numbers. Strategy by the numbers epitomized the predict-and-prepare strategy planning techniques of the 1950s and 1960s. Predict-and-prepare techniques also presumed confidence in the business's future and justified detailed action plans to systematically exploit these expectations. While accurately and systematically forecasting the future now sounds like a futile effort, in the relatively steady slope of postwar business expansion, when the United States was virtually alone in having an intact economy, predicting results in moderate five-year bites—with some accommodation for minor fluctuations—seemed achievable. Bottom-up department or division plans were devised to deliver on top-down sales and revenue decrees.

Predict-and-prepare strategies built momentum through the 1960s and into the early 1970s as U.S. companies launched a diversification binge aimed at sustaining corporate growth and spreading economic risks. Diversification reflected a faith that good general management skills—the product of management science—could readily be transferred, not only to other businesses in the same industry but also to other industries as well. Large, now *horizontally* integrated conglomerates such as Litton, ITT, Textron, and Gulf & Western were the results. ITT's reach, for example, extended to telecommunications, insurance, rental cars, bakeries, and construction.

During the early 1970s, as conglomerate performance lagged, businesses looked for better ways to allocate scarce management resources and to be more systematic and selective in their diversification choices.

One promising alternative was the use of portfolio-planning strategies, a new take on management science analogous to investment portfolio planning. Portfolio planning provided rational quantitative techniques for prioritizing the use of scarce capital—both financial and human— across business categories. Its acceptance of limits and scarcity seemed a way to curtail the excesses of early, indiscriminate diversification choices without abandoning the overall process.

One example of the portfolio-planning concept was the growth-share matrix first introduced by the Boston Consulting Group. The matrix slotted businesses into discrete strategic categories, in this case based on the business's market growth potential (high or low) and its current market share (high or low). Through the four-quadrant model, managers could prioritize businesses from stars (high growth potential, high market share) down to dogs (low growth potential, low market share) and make resource allocations as well as acquisition and divestiture decisions.

While BCG's seemingly simple matrix is, of course, only the bare-bones picture of a more complex evaluation and decision-making process, it and similar models implied that strategic business decisions could be reduced to discrete decision profiles. They seemed to spare business decision makers the interdependent rough-and-tumble of markets, products, customers, and competition. Myopic reliance on the models ran the risk of ignoring potentially lucrative—or disastrous—circumstances waiting outside the analytic confines of the model. Command-and-control strategies had in some ways become remote-control strategies.

And, for the most part, these matrices did not deliver on their stylish promise, stumbling particularly during the mid-1970's oil crisis and the period of ensuing inflation. In terms of business strategies this marked a pendulum swing from the detachment of management science to an increased focus on actual business environments, including the influences of external factors such as industry setting and business competition.

3. Position strategies

The essence of the industry-based position strategies that emerged during the 1980s as the next wave of business strategy thinking is that industry structure determines the nature of industry competition and sets the path and boundaries for the ways that companies conduct business. In other words, industry structure—that is, the number and variety of competitors, product/service pricing, and prevailing technologies, among other factors—has a big impact on what a company *can* do within the universe of what it *might* do. Position strategies accepted limits to the business horizon and emphasized finding the best competitive place within those limits.

According to Harvard Business School professor Michael Porter, the prime mover of this type of thinking, business strategy choices were bounded by the possibilities of the industry and by business environmental forces—for example, current and new competitors and the bargaining powers of suppliers and customers. Successful strategies hinged on getting into the proper industry, and then maneuvering for the proper position within that industry.

Position strategies sort into their own generic strategies matrix (see Exhibit 2-3).[8] To position themselves strategically within the bounds of this matrix, companies confront three fundamental decision options:

Exhibit 2-3. Porter's generic strategies.

	Cost	Differentiation
Broad	**Low cost,** competing in a **broad industry** or market	**Product differentiation,** competing in a **broad industry** or market
Focused	**Low cost,** competing in a **focused segment** of an industry or market	**Product differentiation,** competing in a **focused segment** of an industry or market

1. Whether to compete in a market by adopting a strategy based on (low) *cost advantage*
2. Whether to compete in a market by adopting a strategy based on *differentiation*, for example, competitively distinguishing product/service features or competitively advantageous production, distribution, or support processes
3. Whether to *focus* on a targeted slice of the market, adopting either a *cost advantage* or *differentiation strategy* in competing for that slice

These decisions thus channel companies into one of four possible strategy paths:

1. Cost strategies
2. Differentiation strategies
3. Focus strategies based on cost
4. Focus strategies based on differentiation

Straddling these categories—trying, for example to be both a low-cost business and a differentiated business—portended disaster, leaving companies dangerously stuck in the middle.

4. Competency strategies

Many business leaders found Porter's concepts to be convincing; however, they also found the concepts to be too difficult to practice and, ultimately, too hard to swallow. Prestrategy analysis proved complex and time consuming; making strategy choices was often a wrenching process. And the disciplined set-piece logic of picking an industry, finding a strategic place in that industry, and then playing defense against an array of threats, ran against the grain for U.S. business leaders who cherished the freedom to maneuver, innovate, and even create their own competitive landscapes.

Perhaps for this reason business leaders, who believed the origins of success were embedded in their unique efforts to shape and organize their businesses embraced the emergence during the 1980s of strategy models directed inward on companies and their distinct core capabilities. This was encouraging and motivating for many HR leaders as well because the roots of competitive advantage could be found in talent-based skills, collective learning, and the efforts of business leaders to mobilize them though effective hiring, training, coaching, communication, and motivation. The supporting evidence for this approach came from a mountain of anecdotal evidence and business consulting experience—most visibly via Tom Peters and Robert Waterman's best-selling *In Search of Excellence*[9] and Peter Senge's *The Fifth Discipline*.[10]

These inward-looking strategy approaches, although refreshing, proactive, and scaled to human effort, also proved to be self-congratulatory and naive. Through internal analysis, a company was able to determine its core competencies as well as the collection of products, processes, or technologies at which it excelled over other products, processes, or technologies it might have chosen. But this did not mean these core competencies were necessarily *distinctive*,[11] that is, strengths both for the company as well as strengths when compared with its competitors.

5. Efficiency strategies

In retrospect, the strategies that governed U.S. business marched at an evolutionary pace well through the 1980s. Then, during the late 1980s and early 1990s, businesses faced a series of unforeseen and unprecedented events that canceled all strategy bets. The following came in relatively quick and interdependent succession:

- *The emergence of vastly more competitive global markets for business products and services.* International competition came from low-cost producers, at first indirectly, as overseas companies established local U.S. operations.

- *Domestic deregulation of service-intensive industries* These industries were as varied as transportation, financial services, and telecommunications. International competition became direct, made easier by dropping barriers in communication and transportation.

• *Advances in technology, product cycles, and production.* The competitive market cycle for products and services—from invention through obsolescence—was compressed from generations down to years, months, or even weeks.

• *The relentless pressure to deliver shareholder value.* An investment mantra that compelled corporate managers to think like owners, and launch a continuous assault on fixed costs. The all-out push for operational efficiencies often substituted for strategy.

• *The direct penetration of market forces into cost-heavy internal business operations and processes.* When business leaders dispatched consultants to look under the hoods of their organizations with cost-conscious eyes, the consultants inevitably spotted inefficiencies and proposed radical ways to undo them. There followed widespread, systematic, and continuing initiatives to streamline, outsource, reengineer, or eliminate functions, processes, and departments. Advances in the functionality and availability of information technology also made a huge impact. Hierarchical organizational structures that had been justified as a way to monitor and control the flow of business instructions and information were flattened by IT's speed and twenty-four-by-seven availability.

• *Changes in the structure of business organizations.* The push toward diversification through collections of often-dissimilar businesses did an about face, also compelled by the mantra of shareholder value. Conglomerates spun off subsidiary operations that did not fit their so-called core competencies. Information technology justified the outsourcing of entire categories of work, reversing the trend that had, much earlier in the twentieth century, brought contracted or outsourced work into the business.

• *Changes in business financing.* Conglomerate spin-offs financed through high-interest junk bonds ratcheted up already high debt levels, which further turned up the pressure to increase profits and reduce costs.

The structures and operations of businesses that survived these years were fundamentally reconfigured to be leaner, flatter, cost-driven, process-organized, and customer-focused. Business strategies nearly always boiled down to implementation and operational effectiveness: produce the highest-quality products and services at the lowest cost and improve on best practices.

6. Shorthand strategies

If, in the early 1990s, most business strategies were obsessed with operational details, the explosive new economy of the mid- and late 1990s seemed for a time to challenge the very need for formal strategy. In order to succeed, companies of all sizes and at all stages pursued unanticipated and fleeting opportunities.[12] In this environment, strategy seemed rigid and inflexible—and inevitably outdated by the time it was produced. For many companies, substitutes for strategies came in the form of a few key strategic processes and a handful of simple, easily communicated rules. The rules served to prioritize resource allocations, draw decision boundaries, and time the entry to and exit from markets. Web portal Yahoo!, for example, lived by four "how-to" product innovation rules:

1. Know the priority rank of each product in development.
2. Ensure that every engineer can work every project.
3. Maintain the Yahoo! look and feel in the user interface.
4. Launch products quietly to delay the scrutiny of current and potential competitors.

Similarly, Cisco Systems, the *Fortune* 500 network equipment and infrastructure company that also ranks high on *Fortune*'s list of most admired companies, imposed a 75:75-boundary rule to control its many acquisitions: that is, acquired companies could have at most seventy-five employees, 75 percent of whom had to be engineers.

Many of these were, of course, patched-together mechanisms for coping with an overload of opportunities in what seemed to be an economy of unbounded growth. Because of their immediacy and clarity, some coping mechanisms substituted adequately for strategy during the short term and on the upside. (*Coping* probably describes the approach to talent acquisition of many companies during the talent wars.)

However, when the capital sources were eventually no longer willing to settle for concepts and unbridled growth, but instead demanded more traditional operations, revenue, and profit results, more than shorthand strategies were needed. Indeed, some of these shorthand strategies—witness the events at Enron where, for example, commodities traders were given considerable latitude in pursuing new risk opportunities provided each trader "report(ed) a daily profit-and-loss statement"—may have played no small part in accelerating the unraveling of the new economy.[13]

7. Customer strategies

In close retrospect, the mid- to late 1990s seemed to be an era of almost effortless business. In some ways, it was a repeat of the 1950s, although with 1990's giddiness replacing 1950's buttoned-down confidence. By contrast, early in this new decade circumstances point to conditions more reminiscent of the 1970's energy crisis and inflation or global competition in the 1980s: unsteady markets, scarce capital, shareholder impatience, the possible reemergence of global turbulence, and the realization that technologies that once fueled economic growth have become low-price commodities.

They also seem to point to a new business challenge: the new target in these lean times seems to be the customer. Meaning, that is, the customer at all levels: the corporate customers of suppliers as well the consumers of corporate products and services—not to mention customers for intrabusiness services such as HR.

Customers have already benefited from the increased number of competitors resulting from globalization—for example, the Big Three automakers of the 1950s, 1960s, and early 1970s are now the Global 25. Now there are accelerating circumstances:

- Customers are continuing to benefit from increased productivity's ability to deliver surplus goods.
- Customers are better informed by new, mostly electronic sources of information and thus better able to relentlessly comparison shop; in effect, cost-led pricing has been replaced by price-led costing.
- Customers have the advantage of compressed product cycles that provide a continuous carousel of new product choices and a savage discounting of aging ones.
- Customers face an increasingly varied and attractive array of time-dependent product choices—in entertainment, leisure, and travel—without much additional time to experience them.

Against this new backdrop of competition and in this once again uncertain economic climate, businesses at all levels seem to be turning once again to purposeful strategies. Not because strategies are easier but because strategies are the hard-thought competitive differentiators in these sorts of times. (See Exhibit 2-4.) Perhaps most emblematic of the change—the merging of strategy with customer needs—was the direction that IBM ultimately took under Louis Gerstner's leadership. As Gerstner recounted in an interview with *The New York Times*: "We were going to build this company from the customer back, not from the company out. That was the big message from my first six months in the company, that the company was going to be driven from the marketplace."[14]

New business strategy landscape

What forms are these strategies taking—and not taking? We can review them in terms of the models we've just developed:

1. *Integration.* Vertical (all things under one umbrella) integration strategies are too costly and cumbersome, and rely too much on

Exhibit 2-4. Business strategies concepts.

Strategy	Unifying concept(s)	Historic events and economic conditions	Era
1. Integration strategies	• Vertical integration: control of materials and process from raw material to customer • Manage growth/complexity through multi-layered organizations	Lack of government regulation re: competition	Pre-WWII
2. Planning strategies	• Management science: quantitative management and analytic techniques • Detailed action plans to systematically exploit these expectations • Diversification reflected faith that general management skills could readily be transferred within and between industries • Portfolio planning provided rational quantitative techniques for prioritizing the use of scarce capital • More systematic/selective in diversification choices	Unhindered growth of U.S. postwar economy	1940s
			1950s
			1960s
		• Slowing growth • Energy crisis • Inflation	1970s
3. Position strategies	• Industry structure determines nature of industry competition and sets path/boundaries for the ways that companies conduct business • Getting into the right industry, and then maneuvering for the right position within that industry • Strategies based on cost or differentiation		1980s

	Era	Context	Strategy	Description
4.	1980s	• Emergence of more competitive global markets • Deregulation of service-intensive industries • Advances in technology • Pressure to deliver shareholder value	Competency strategies	• Strategy models directed inward on companies and their distinct core competencies/capabilities • Competitive advantage could be found in talent-based skills, collective learning, and the efforts of business leaders
5.			Efficiency strategies	• Continuous assault on fixed costs • Push for operational efficiencies through quality, process reengineering • Businesses fundamentally reconfigured: leaner, flatter, cost-driven, process-organized
6.	1990s	• Explosive "new economy" • Unanticipated and fleeting opportunities • Economy of unbounded growth	Shorthand strategies	• Strategies rigid and inflexible—and inevitably outdated by the time they were produced • Substitutes for strategies sometimes in the form of a few key strategic processes and simple, easily communicated rules • Mechanisms for coping with an overload of opportunities
7.	2000s	• Economic slowdown	Customer strategies	• Customer value propositions • Hands-on strategies developed and executed close to the customer

noncompetitive competencies to be the current basis for competitive customer strategies. Vertical integration, according to consultant and academic Michael Hammer, has become *virtual* integration—in other words, a return to preconglomerate days. Cisco Systems, for example, limits its focus to two strategic activities: developing state-of-the art product and maintaining close customer relationships. Nearly all the intervening steps, including product manufacturing and distribution, are left to outside partners.[15] And the same is true for other technology and telecommunications brands such as Hewlett Packard, Dell, and Nortel. More generally, business organizations increasingly look for opportunities to outsource parts and sometimes all of what they see as noncore functions, including administrative services, IT, and HR. Where integration strategies created enterprises that might be compared to organisms held together by rigid shells, today's strategies and enterprises are designed around flexible skeletons of information and relationships.[16]

Business strategies are also organized closer to customers. It is unusual for even moderately large corporations to be organized around major functional departments with detailed strategies developed and directed rigidly from the top. Instead, to attract and service a wider diversity of customers, businesses have continued shifting strategy decisions and accountabilities away from the corporate center and out to strategic business units (SBUs), self-contained businesses run by general managers, which provide certain products and services to certain customers. Not coincidentally, the SBU business strategies are more direct and sensitive to results.

2. *Planning.* Strategies are more hands-on and are the direct products of visionary entrepreneurs and management teams. Separate planning staffs, elaborate planning processes, and detailed revenue forecasts have fallen victim to combinations of business velocity, business forecasting uncertainty, and the compression and trimming of corporate staffs. Strategy planning based on elaborate steps, checklists, and techniques has given way to strategy designing:

- Formulation of clear, simple, and unique strategies
- More emphasis on execution than formulation
- Fewer people exclusively involved in strategy planning, many more involved in strategy execution

The other significant feature of planning-based business strategies—long-term forecasts of future costs, prices, or revenues—gets little emphasis and less credibility. Such forecasts usually end up being wrong. Strategies have become projections of competitive advantage—that is, profitability regardless of cost, price, or revenue conditions.

3. *Positioning*. Position strategies also serve well as customer strategies, although with more variations and competitive edge. For one thing, nearly all position strategies have little choice but to be competitive on cost. In addition, companies craft customer strategies that—ignoring admonitions not to be "stuck in the middle"—feature additional competitive features beyond price and niche. For example, Southwest Airlines, which competes and succeeds famously in a niche market for no-frills, low-cost direct flight transportation, competes not only on cost but also through world-class customer service. It claims aggressively that it is in the customer service business, but just happens to be delivering customer service via air transportation.

The hearts and souls of business strategies are their customer value propositions, that is, how the business differentiates itself from competitors to attract new customers and build relationships with existing customers. The best and most successful of these convey a compelling and distinguishing logic, so it is hardly surprising that some of these are in the retailing sector—*Fortune* 500 general merchandiser Wal-Mart, for example, profiles its strategy succinctly with: "Always low prices . . . always." And, as another example, specialty outdoor clothing retailer Patagonia unabashedly appeals to the "dirtbag within" of its customers.

4. *Competencies*. Business strategies pay attention to *distinctive* core competencies. Considerable energy and attention are directed toward choosing and doing the things that companies do well—both compared

with the other things they might do and how their performance of these competencies stacks up against competitor performance of the same competencies. *Business Week* listed core competencies as one of the five major schools of thought that would be guiding twenty-first-century managers.[17]

5. *Efficiencies.* Operational initiatives such as reengineering and total quality management, once the backbone of efficiency strategies, while still important, no longer pass strategic muster because they seldom are distinguishing features of company strategies. Best practices are now about what every business needs to do to stay in business. Strategies are about doing different things or doing them in different ways.

6. *Shorthand strategies.* The immediacy and clarity of simple how-to and boundary rules that characterized many new economy coping strategies continue to have a welcome editorial impact on what were often vague, indistinguishable, and sometimes numbing mission and vision statements of previous eras. Of course, strategy brevity and clarity are hardly unique to the new economy. The best example is former General Electric CEO Jack Welch's concise strategy/admonition to "fix, sell or close" any GE business not number one or two in its global market. It is clear that in the customer era, more businesses are striving to hone and simplify their strategic messages.

Business strategy's management cycles

Despite what we've said about strategy being customer focused, hands on, and less reliant on assured, long-term forecasts, when you visualize business strategy formation it is still easy to imagine a formal process of precise rules, procedures, and time frames. While most businesses have some type of formal strategy planning process, at least on paper, the reality is that it comes in all shapes and sizes. Large multidivisional businesses may need and use a complex strategy formation process to coordinate corporate, business unit, and functional strategies. Strategy formation for a small entrepreneurial company may be the product of ongoing informal discussions by company founders.

Regardless of how strategy gets formed it usually blends strategic intentions and strategic adaptation to events. It is also usually a combination of annual and longer-term cycles.

Annual cycle

Every business inevitably confronts its strategies at budgeting time. This annual cycle is apt to have three components:

1. *Top-down strategy.* A business-level review of business direction against near-term business environment; a review of current customers and competitors; identification of the most serious market threats and best opportunities; and the conversion/communication of this analysis into priorities and quantified objectives.
2. *Bottom-up action planning.* The process of converting company-level objectives into division, department, or function objectives; action plans to achieve them; and preliminary budgets.
3. *Budgeting.* The tangible allocation of financial resources to meet goals and objectives.

Longer-term cycle

This annual planning cycle is often part of a broader and longer-term strategy management cycle. This cycle (see Exhibit 2-5), again conceptually, consists of four stages, which precede, incorporate, and extend beyond the annual cycle:

1. *Internal and external scanning.* Internally, a scan of business structure, culture, resources, and capabilities. Externally, consideration of a range of circumstances and events important to the business: legislative, legal, economic, industry, competitor, and others.
2. *Strategy formation.* The stage that produces the top-down strategies by way of formal expressions such as a mission statement or

Exhibit 2-5. Business strategies management cycle.

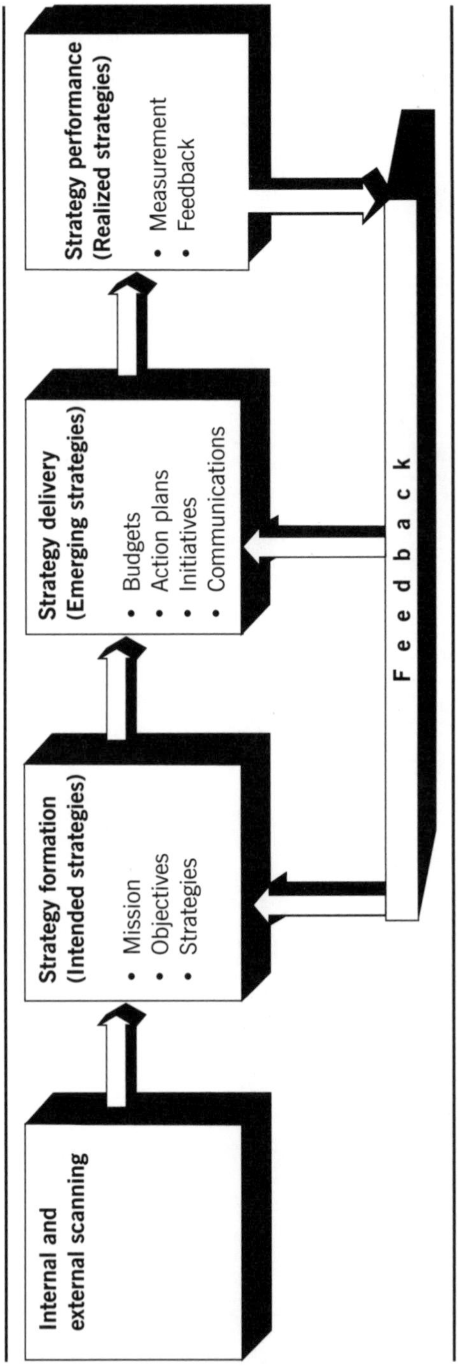

customer value proposition, key objectives, and the strategies for accomplishing them. These are the strategies that are intended.

3. *Strategy delivery.* The stage that encompasses annual bottom-up action planning and budgeting. These are the strategies that emerge based on strategic behaviors and adaptation to events.

4. *Strategy performance, measurement, and feedback.* Ongoing measurement, evaluation, and control of strategy delivery. These are the strategies that result—the realized strategies.

While the horizon of confidence for this longer strategy cycle has, for most industries in most markets, decidedly shortened from the more stable era of planning strategies, the time frame should be at least three to five years. During this time frame, as depicted in Exhibit 2-6 on page 54, the broader strategy management cycle both drives and is driven (through the feedback of events and operating results) by the annual strategy planning cycle.

Exhibit 2-7, on page 55, presents this strategy landscape in terms of time frames, directions, actions, and outcomes. You can see that business strategies—paired with talent strategies—have their place in the middle range at a stage beyond short-term actions and outcomes, yet short of business visions. Strategies are longer term but also tangible and hands on.

Next, in Chapter 3, we look at the place of talent and talent strategies within this landscape.

Exhibit 2-6. Strategy management cycle and annual strategy planning cycle.

Exhibit 2-7. Business strategies landscape.

	Time frame			
	Current (3–12 months)	Short-term (1–3 years)	Long-term (3–10 years)	Open-ended
Directions	• Strategy communication	• Customer value proposition • Strategic intent • Success factors • Alignment	• Strategy design • Market foresight • Business image • Distinctive competencies	• Strategic vision • Mission • Core values
Actions	• Performance plans • Decision rules • Processes	• Budgets • Process initiatives • Channeling resources to distinctive competencies	• Business strategies • Talent strategies	Competency building
Outcomes (measures)	Reporting metrics • Operational measures • Financial measures	Performance goals • Financial measures • Balanced measures • Process improvement measures	Business objectives	

Notes

1. Michael Hammer, *Agenda* (New York: Crown Business, 2001), p. 245.

2. Of considerable comfort, though, should be the fact that subtlety and context also make it difficult for competitors and potential competitors to successfully copy the strategy. This no-shortcuts "path dependency" creates a barrier to entry. Would-be competitors must themselves live the experience through which the strategy developed to be able to successfully compete.

3. Robert S. Kaplan and David P. Norton, "Having Trouble with Your Strategy? Then Map It," *Harvard Business Review* (September–October, 2000), pp. 167–176.

4. Writing in the Spring 1999 issue of *Sloan Management Review*, two Canadian university business professors, Henry Mintzburg and Joseph Lampel, counted ten separate strategy schools: three *prescriptive* (or "ought") and seven *descriptive* (or "is").

5. Robert Grant, *Contemporary Strategy Analysis* (Cambridge, MA: Basil Blackwell, 1991), p. 15.

6. Hammer, p. 199.

7. Steve Lohr, "He Loves to Win. At IBM, He Did," *The New York Times*, March 10, 2002, p. B11.

8. Michael Porter, *Competitive Strategy* (New York: The Free Press, 1980), Ch. 2.

9. Tom Peters and Robert Waterman, *In Search of Excellence* (New York: Warner Books, 1984).

10. Peter M. Senge, *The Fifth Discipline: The Art and Practice of the Learning Organization* (New York: Currency/Doubleday, 1994).

11. David J. Collins and Cynthia A. Montgomery, "Competing on Resources: Strategy in the 1990's," *Harvard Business Review*, July–August, 1985, pp. 118–128.

12. Kathleen M. Eisenhardt and Donald N. Sull, "Strategy As Simple Rules," *Harvard Business Review*, January 2001, pp. 107–117.

13. Ibid., p. 114

14. Lohr, p. B11.

15. Hammer, p. 212.

16. Peter F. Drucker, ''The Information Executives Truly Need'' in *Harvard Business Review on Measuring Corporate Performance* (Boston: Harvard Business School Press, 1998), p. 23.

17. The others are empowerment, learning organization, reengineering, and organizational architecture.

CHAPTER 3

☑ VALUING TALENT

N 1956 WILLIAM WHYTE'S BOOK, *The Organization Man*, defined the archetypal U.S. business professional: He worked for a large company, offering loyalty in exchange for job security and upward mobility. He had average workweeks of fifty to sixty hours, working four out of five weeknights. His basic motivation for working long hours was because his ego demanded it, not because he was specifically ordered to. He worked for an organization with little room for virtuosos: In other words, he knew that to stay and succeed he must be able to work with other people.

Most important, the Organization Man's identity was defined by where he worked and what he did for a living. He saw an ultimate harmony between himself and the organization. "(T)he goals of the individual and the goals of the organization will work out to be one and the same. . . . They have an implicit faith that The Organization will be as interested in making use of their best qualities as they are themselves, and thus, with equanimity, they can entrust the resolution of their destiny to The Organization . . . (H)is relationship with The Organization is to be for keeps."[1]

To Whyte the term *organization man* had a distinct meaning. (In Whyte's 1956 book, *organization man* was clearly not intended as a gender-neutral term.) Organization Men were not production workers, nor were they "white-collar people in the usual, clerk sense of the word."[2] Employees in such categories only worked *for* the organization. By contrast, Organization Men, through their level of commitment, attachment, and identification, *belonged* to the organization as well.

Working for/belonging to

This working for/belonging to distinction is important to understanding how talent fits into business strategies. For example, working *for* implies one level of commitment, while belonging *to* implies a much deeper, presumably mutual commitment. As we consider today our own roles in business organizations, how would we best describe them? Do we see ourselves just in a job, merely working for a company? Or do we see ourselves being an integral part—belonging to—an organization? And what do our answers say about our levels of work effort, commitment, and engagement? If we say that we are merely working for a business, how do we feel? Bad? Do we blame the organization or ourselves? If we feel comfortable with the "working for" designation, yet work fifty to sixty hours per week, plus weeknights, at our own initiative, how do we feel then?

These questions become even more interesting if you're involved in talent and talent strategies issues. As you think about the talent in your organization or the talent you need to acquire and keep, how does this working for/belonging to distinction play out in the ability of your business to meet its strategy objectives? Although we'll cover this issue in more detail later on, I think most of us have a sneaking suspicion that, in recent years and with some notable exceptions, the balance of workplace involvement—if placed on a "for/to" scale—has tipped, psychologically at least, to the "for" side. If we believe this is so, and if we accept Chapter 2's points about business-strategy trends such as:

- More focus on customer-based strategies
- Simpler strategies that depend heavily on execution and the involvement of more people in order to succeed
- Reliance on distinctive competencies, many of them embodied in intangibles, including people

then we've got to believe that devising distinctive and successful talent strategies will involve narrowing huge gaps between business's expectations from talent and talent's commitment to business.

The history of talent

Whyte scrutinized the Organization Man at a time when U.S. business strategies were defined by centralization, vertical integration, diversification, and strategic planning.[3] This was an era of confident post–World War II economic prosperity with corporate functions, departments, and divisions expanding considerably. Organization Man's commitment to the Organization had at least something to do with the bounty of opportunities—organizational charts where the connecting lines appeared to rise in parallel, instead of converging abruptly near the top.[4]

The Organization Man describes the role of talent in the context of particular strategies at a particular time. Was it always that way? How and why has it changed since? What can we expect from it in the future? How the Organization and its customers value talent and how talent views the Organization and itself are important considerations for business strategies. What we're concerned with in this chapter is how the Organization Man (and Woman) came to be, what they've been doing since, and finally, what we think they'll be doing in the future.

Free agent nation

During the latter stages of the industrial economy and up to the years immediately following World War I, U.S. employment arrangements were more farm-based than factory- or office-based. Employment was casual, contractual, and outsourced. Employers avoided practically all the risks and commitments of employment while workers shouldered nearly all the risks and lacked most of the commitments. Many of these arrangements were economically precarious for most workers and notoriously brutal and exploitive as well. And for many years these circumstances were the targets of religious, political, and journalistic efforts aimed at reversing them.

By the time of the Industrial Revolution, dramatic changes to the ways work was organized and workers deployed had already occurred. Manufacturing output had increased by orders of magnitude through division of labor, a paradigm-shifting concept first advanced by eighteenth-century British philosopher and economist Adam Smith in *The Wealth of Nations*.

Smith discovered that specialists performing single steps in a manufacturing process could achieve vastly more output than identical numbers of generalists. Division of labor, first applied to the simple fabrication of pins, had, by the early twentieth century, invaded nearly all aspects of plant and office work. Twentieth-century vertical integration strategies became possible in part because of the division of labor: the ability of businesses to organize and harness the output of workers performing highly fragmented work. In a way, division of labor made up the building blocks of organization pyramids, although these building blocks were added at the bottom rather than at the top. During good economic times, businesses grew by constantly adding entry-level talent to the pyramid's base.

The birth of productivity

Division of labor was more of a boon to businesses than to workers: It often meant numbingly repetitive work for long hours in spartan, even horrid conditions. But it was less altruism than the efficiency needs of vertically integrated businesses that triggered substantial, and in many ways, beneficial changes in both the setting and technology of work. Among these needs was ensuring a reserve of company-specific, higher-level skills to better coordinate long-term planning, accomplish more complex production tasks, and sustain growth.

The employment-based means toward this end were varied. Better pay was one tactic. For example, Ford Motor's annual employee turnover rate plummeted from 370 percent to 54 percent with the near doubling of pay to $5 per day in 1913. (And, not incidentally, it put Ford's output of Model T's within the purchasing power of assembly-line talent.)

The removal of an individual supervisor's power in hiring and firing was another change. This discretion became centralized under the control of a newly formed company employment or personnel department.

The personnel department's charter was to help meet the company's efficiency needs through improved selection processes. Driving this charter were the findings of the so-called scientific management movement whose objectives were the improvement of manufacturing operations through systematic engineering methods.[5] Scientific management used the division of labor concept as a departure point for an entirely new way of organizing and directing work.

Among scientific management's premises was that work performance improved by systematically matching employee characteristics to job conditions and requirements. The steps to enhance this match included:

- Careful job design based on component tasks
- Determining the best procedures for performing these tasks

- Defining employee characteristics best adapted to tasks and procedures

Scientific management principles represented, for business, the first reasons to value the unique contributions of talent.

Scientific management also revealed a totally new work concept: productivity. While division of labor was about increasing work output, it departed little from the centuries-old assumption that the only real distinctions among workers were skills and effort. Production, even organized by specialization, depended on how long and how hard people worked: Hard workers produced more, lazy workers less.

Scientific management added employee characteristics as a crucial factor; its engineers toiled through exhaustive analysis to determine the one best way for workers to perform jobs and tasks.[6] The means to ensure this match between employees and the best ways were standardized selection tests originally devised by the military for recruit placement purposes. Tests enabled employers to choose the right person for a particular job. Once the employee was in place, pay incentives (often piece- or production-rates) motivated the employee to perform the job well. Applying scientific management methods, at least in manual work settings, had huge payoffs. One estimate is a fifty-fold increase in manual work productivity from the first decade of the application of scientific management through the end of the twentieth century.[7]

The top-down counterpart to bottom-up scientific management was administrative science. If scientific management dismantled and reassembled jobs in the interest of work performance efficiency, administrative science—pioneered by French industrialist Henri Fayol—attempted to design the best organization architecture in which to structure these scientifically constructed jobs and the talent that performed them. Fayol's principles for general business management and organizational structure included defining concepts such as unity of command, span of control, and centralized decision making. Although they advocated fair treatment of talent (including fair pay and lifetime employment), they were also authoritative and tightly structured.

The talent machine

Division of labor, scientific management, and administrative science combined to form a model of talent deployment ideally matched to the vertical integration strategies of pre- and postwar U.S. enterprise. The architecture—or the system—was the pyramid hierarchy of the corporation. The working parts—or the content—were the arrangement of jobs.

For certain talent categories—what Whyte described as workers and white-collar people "in the usual, clerk sense of the word"—this meant task- and specification-based jobs into which employees were sorted. Within these categories, the architecture provided a consistent mechanism to build and deepen the talent bench: policies of promotion from within. Internal promotion processes were often based on job classification practices and arrangements that grouped similarly skilled jobs into career hierarchies or ladders. Workers in classified jobs could learn the skills and gain the experience needed to climb to the next rung of the promotional ladder. The results, advocates of job classification argued, were that skills would increase, employees would stay longer as they aspired to climb a career ladder, and, perhaps most important, the hope of internal promotion motivated employees to be both committed and productive.

For the Organization Men (eventually to include Organization Women), the Organization's leadership and management talent, there was an analogous but more intensive promotion from within process. Talent at this level in effect had the employer and the employer's identity as their careers. College graduates signed on, were incubated and trained by the Organization, and then moved through a series of lateral and promotional jobs in different departments and functions, and often in different locations. While they inevitably filled functional specialty roles—in sales or marketing or finance or personnel—they typically did not attach themselves to professions except that of generalists for their businesses.

Yet, even among the cadres of Organization Men and Women belonging to businesses, there was division and fragmentation of work. With the creation of decentralized divisions, the complementary emergence of management science techniques, and the parceling of Organization Men and Women among divisions, executive expertise shifted away from disciplines such as engineering and manufacturing and toward finance—the number-intensive skills needed to monitor and evaluate performance across varied types of business.

Management work became even more fragmented during the era of planning strategies—the period during which Whyte conducted his studies of business organizations. Investment-style, portfolio-planning decisions about which businesses and markets to enter; how much capital should be allocated; and the financial results to be expected required the analysis and legwork of large staffs of controllers, auditors, and planners. Talent efforts were devoted to information collection, data crunching, financial analysis, results reporting, and interventions to adjust business plans and operational management.

What appeared clear and seamless from the outside caused some trouble on the inside. Industrial engineers and managers often forgot that the running parts for this tidy architecture were, after all, people. The overly impersonal aspects of management science and administrative science ran into predictable resentment and resistance. Emerging from this backlash, in stages through the 1930s, 1940s, and 1950s, were human relations concepts and practices designed to respond to the interpersonal needs of people in work organizations: communications, interpersonal relations, and leadership behavior. The practices were not ends in themselves; they were justified as a means to improve productivity. While some employers applied human relations techniques as a thin veneer to their regular ways of doing business, many invested heavily for a number of years in human relations training for their supervisors and managers.

Status quo

This blending of scientific management, administrative science, and human relations described the talent side of the Organization portrayed in *The Organization Man*. Work fragmentation, increasing productivity, and the cushioning human relations efforts characterized work from the shop floor through the back office and up to the executive suite.

Long-term employment relationships and internal career movement were work-life features benefiting both employer and employee. Employees got the advantages of more predictable and less one-sided and onerous work arrangements, while employers realized three key benefits:

1. They could afford to invest in training, knowing that their investments would be rewarded through improved long-term performance. Much of this investment was directed toward procedural or administrative skills that met the organization's particular internal needs and could not readily be transferred to other organizations.
2. Employment security reaped returns in the form of employee loyalty and commitment.
3. The possibility of internal promotion provided broad-based motivation at relatively low cost. Many employees could aspire to promotion and would perform accordingly, often in roles for which the employer rather than a profession was the career. Employees aspired to promotions in steep organizational pyramids where only a handful could realistically make it to the top.[8] Nevertheless, many behaved and performed as if they were heading there.

While this stable, insulated, and predictable employment environment probably reached its high point in the 1950s, it endured more or less intact through the 1960s, 1970s, and early 1980s. Although there were occasional upheavals, and good employment times and bad, the prevailing work/career model across a range of industries and business sizes was long-term employment. The basic features of this model from talent's perspective were:

- A stable and reciprocal employer/employee relationship characterized by jobs with defined titles, duties, and responsibilities.

- Structured (and internally equitable) pay arrangements geared to a base salary (with perhaps some moderate incentives) and standard employee benefits.
- A narrow variety of employment arrangements, mostly full-time; factory-, office-, or executive suite-bound; exclusive and uninterrupted.
- Career path progressions usually channeled through employer-specific disciplines and governed by length of service with awards and privileges for longer-term service.
- Relatively little movement between companies; for supervisors, middle managers, and many employees who had received lengthy firm-specific training and work experience, employment barriers to entry in other industries or even in competing companies were formidable. That training and experience, while of considerable internal value to their current employer, had relatively little value to other employers.
- Pay-for-performance arrangements that actually bore little relation to business performance and merit pay practices that tended not to differentiate employee pay adjustments.

The employment pact based on these features could reinforce itself for a career lifetime—the higher one climbed in a company, the greater the rewards and the stronger the incentive to stay and try for more. For many employees the company was synonymous with profession and career.

This is not to say that employment relationships were always smooth. They could be contentious, adversarial, and sometimes even feudal, with worker employment sometimes administered at arm's length through unions and collective bargaining agreements. But the concept was the same—indeed, collective bargaining arrangements made the employment relationship even more rigid for the 15 million or so unionized employees in the United States, with most employment-related decisions controlled by job classification and seniority.

Taking down the pyramids

During the business strategy eras that encompassed company positioning and then company competencies, the Organization Man model
began to show cracks. Positioning strategies made many companies confront what really distinguished them to their customers and within their
markets. If it was to be cost, they realized that organization hierarchies
did not come cheap. If it was to be some other competitive factor—
customer service or speed of new product development, for example—
they began to realize that fragmented work winding through organizational layers was a hindrance. Key competencies such as autonomy,
entrepreneurship, customer intimacy, being hands-on, and loose-tight
management were hard to achieve within rigid pyramid structures.

But ultimately it was the same series of economic upheavals that
generated the efficiency strategies of the late 1980s and early 1990s—
more competitive global markets, the IT revolution, and the relentless
pressure to deliver shareholder value—that upended the model once
and for all.[9] The combined effects of these upheavals were to systematically unwind the machinery of U.S. business employment, eventually
putting in its place an open, unruly, and competitive employment marketplace. While many skeletons of old employment arrangements (job
titles and salary grades, for example) remained in place and some employers and employees continued to act as if nothing revolutionary had
occurred, something revolutionary had indeed occurred.

An important rationale for building business structures in hierarchical pyramids—in addition to providing employees with internal promotional and long-term skill building opportunities—had been the need
to monitor, channel, and control the flow of essential business instructions and information. With new advances, IT substituted as the methodology for managing organization controls, often providing the
twenty-four-by-seven means of displacing middle managers and admin-
istrators. Information technology also provided the technological means
for outsourcing entire categories of work, reversing the trend that had,
earlier in the twentieth century, brought contracted or outsourced work

into the business. When supplemented by the other techniques for reducing costs, IT paved the way for job cuts: Workforces and the redundant employment architecture were an organization's most visible and dispensable fixed costs.

Citing the relentless and Darwinian pressures of market competition, employers—first in a whisper and then in a booming chorus—disavowed their job security commitments to employees. Companies as prominent and people-intensive as GE, Apple, IBM, and AT&T began to explicitly signal to their employees that they could no longer economically justify old arrangements, and that individuals should assume personal responsibility for their skills, their employment, and their careers.

Just as business had not created the traditional employment model through benevolence, it did not break the compact out of spite. Nonetheless, employment and talent career management essentially moved outside the bounds of individual businesses to become market-mediated processes.

Talent on the open market

The emergence of the employment marketplace during the 1980s and 1990's has been one of the most important business developments of this generation. The marketplace has fundamentally altered the internal talent policies and deployment practices of most employers. Companies have become increasingly less able to define their own, unique employment relationships, while talent, for its part, has had to scramble to assemble careers tied to skills and professions rather than employer classifications and promotion ladders.[10]

Employment quickly morphed to a market-driven process involving talent buyers and sellers with market advantage alternating between them. Constant and open negotiation of the employment relationship has largely displaced discretionary practices such as equity-based compensation, employer-financed training, career ladders, and promotions—practices originally conceived to retain employees, develop needed skills, and ensure commitment.

Talent takes it on the chin

The demise of the traditional employment model in the midst of the early 1990s economic downturn at first left legions of employees dazed and disadvantaged in the marketplace. The employment landscape changed abruptly and unexpectedly; assumptions about security and lifetime employment literally seemed to be there one day and gone the next. And many workers lacked the skills demanded by the new talent market: Their training and expertise were either too employer specific; or their talents were weighted toward the analysis, coordination, communication, and intermediation skills of administration and middle management, which were now virtually wiped out by heavy doses of IT, reengineering, and pyramid flattening.[11]

For many workers the impact was devastating and career ending, especially for legions of older employees short of retirement. But for others the disadvantage, while painful, was temporary. In the mid-1990s businesses once again became competitive and efficient with mounting needs for talent—but no longer had internal talent reserves to draw upon. Now it became talent's turn to sample the advantages of the competitive employment marketplace.

You want loyalty? Get a dog

During the new economy surge, skilled talent stood out as one of the few real competitive advantages for customer-driven business strategies. Ironically, the need for highly skilled talent resulted from a decade's worth of efficiency-based strategy initiatives. For example, process-reengineering initiatives created more complex jobs requiring more judgment, a greater breadth of skills, and better decision making at all organization levels. The expansion and proliferation of IT demanded a constant and climbing intake of entirely new levels of technically skilled talent.

Possessing physical capital such as equipment and computer systems no longer set competitors apart. Equipment and computer systems proved to be commodities routinely available to all competitors and within the budgets of most. Instead, it became the capability to use that capital effectively that seemed to make the difference. A company that lost capital assets while retaining its access to key talent had a better prospect of recovery than did a company that lost access to talent while keeping its assets. Having reliable access to skilled, turn-key talent to operate and leverage assets employed in end-to-end processes could represent a unique competitive advantage.

Consider some of the key ways companies maneuver to compete in customer–focused product and service markets:

- They target market niches with finely tailored products and services that potential competitors overlook.
- They use smaller production runs and processes that are more flexible.
- They compress development and product delivery times.
- They try to emphasize and enhance the service component of their business offerings.
- They organize team-based projects in flattened cross-functional organization structures.
- They rely on outsourcing and subcontracting for needs outside of core company competencies.
- In the search for the right blends of skills, they increase the frequency of restructuring-based dismissals and hires.

The talent outcome of all this was that a company's business competencies increasingly resided within individual employees rather than in organizational systems.[12] These competencies were as diverse and specialized as software development, database administration, project management, product marketing, solution sales, account management, help-desk administration, financial reporting, and customer relations. Competencies crucial for supporting new market essentials were speed, innovation, short cycle times, quality, brand recognition, and customer satisfaction.

The ability to possess these specific, complex skills during the windows of market opportunity when they were most needed put many workers in the driver's seat. It could keep them in that seat if they stayed mindful of two key factors:

1. Being able to adequately forecast and prepare for needed skills
2. Understanding that customer relation skills (a superset of the intrapersonal skills required of the Organization Man) are doubly crucial across professions and industries—for quickly landing employment and for successfully fulfilling the increased share of customer-facing job content

As the end of the second millennium neared, with the U.S. and global economies thriving on the basis of ready capital and innovations in technology, electronic communications, and finance, talent was at a premium. But trained, skilled human capital was no longer a captive resource in the ways it had been. When employers walked away from the notion of job security, training opportunities, and promotions, talent took them at their word and adapted. The best of them learned to take responsibility for their own careers.

These new talent mercenaries were aided by technology, particularly the Internet, which increased the availability and quality of market information. They could go to career sites and job boards to passively— and for the most part anonymously—learn about the market. They could apply for market opportunities directly or merely test the waters. They could benchmark their career progress, experience, and skills against what the market was looking for. By touring job boards, participating in chat rooms, or surfing Internet portals specializing in salary and benefit information, they could compare their pay against going rates—by profession, geography, industry, or career stage. In fact, they could do most of the things and find out most of the information that had formerly been the near-exclusive province of HR.

With the mid-1990s market advantage pendulum swinging from employment buyers to employment sellers, many sellers had also become free agents who saw both lifestyle and economic advantages in working for—not belonging to—organizations. They had learned to look out for themselves and had shifted their allegiances to their skills, networks, and accomplishments. Consider these data points from a summer 2001 study of the employment marketplace by the consulting firm Towers Perrin:

- Fifty-six percent of workers in the study reported being in the job market in some capacity, either actively looking or "job scanning," and being open to considering new opportunities or other offers.
- Job scanners keep their eyes and ears open in various ways: 40 percent reported having talked with friends at other companies, 36 percent having researched job postings on Web sites, and 30 percent having talked with a former colleague who had recently left the company.

Traditional companies, with long-term or lifetime employment, had been communities of sorts. Free agency represents an erosion of commitment matching the erosion of stability that gave rise to it. In other words, the balance had noticeably tipped—even for managers and high-level professionals—from "belonging to" to "working for."

Valuing talent: four realities

In the new landscape of employment and talent, employment bargaining power shifts back and forth based on market conditions. Memory about the talent market past tends to be short, just as confident projections about its future tend to stumble as the future arrives.

For several years, employment sellers had an almost unprecedented upper hand, creating a temporary, distorted reality that played out through unbounded recruiting, ballooning head counts, and unsustainable pay arrangements. But employment buyers who think they are only now first tasting market advantages are wrong. As we've seen, market-driven employment began as an employer-dictated response to global market conditions and the relentless cost-cutting pursuit of shareholder value. And before that, during the era of the Organization Man, employers set the terms and conditions. We should be careful, from the current vantage point, about locking ourselves into assumptions and arrangements that are at best (or at worst) temporary.

Chapter 1 stressed that so-called baked in demographic changes—an exit of baby boomers systematically exceeding the entrance of younger skilled replacements—portend an economy-wide talent shortage in the second decade of this century. Although these demographic changes are undeniable, their projected impact should come with an all-things-being-equal caveat. For example, look at today's most important businesses and news trends. (As of this writing, my list would include the war against terrorism, layoffs and economic recession, and the collapse of Enron). Then look back over the past three years and ask yourself whether you could have forecasted—or wildly imagined—any or all of them. The point is that unforeseen events and circumstances inevitably intervene and interact in unforeseen ways.

Another thing to keep in mind is that employers view talent issues through the prism of their current and expected business needs. Their talent concerns boil down to obtaining the talent needed for a particular time at the price they were willing or able to pay. Employers' problems are not the entire employment market. Employers, for example, do not face demographic shortages; instead they face shortages of skills to accomplish the work that drives their strategies and competitiveness.

Acknowledging these limitations, we can still benefit from what we know about business strategies (past and present) and the valuing of talent (past and present). (See Exhibit 3-1.) Before turning to the discussion about the building and delivery of talent strategies in Part II, we can refocus these binocular views to describe four realities that intensify the convergence of talent, markets, and business strategies.

Reality #1: Talent is knowledge

The talent categories Whyte describes in *The Organization Man* have increasingly less in common with the present or future. Nor do the tasks,

Exhibit 3-1. Talent history.

Strategy	Unifying concept(s)	Talent history	Era
1. Integration strategies	• Vertical integration: control of materials and process from raw material to customer • Manage growth/complexity through multi-layered organizations	• Division of labor • Scientific management • Administrative science	Pre-WWII
2. Planning strategies	• Management science: quantitative management and analytic techniques	• Human relations movement • Organization Man	1940s
	• Detailed action plans to systematically exploit these expectations		1950s
	• Diversification reflected faith that general management skills could readily be transferred within and between industries		1960s
	• Portfolio planning provided rational quantitative techniques for prioritizing the use of scarce capital • More systematic/selective in diversification choices		1970s
3. Position strategies	• Industry structure determines nature of industry competition and sets path/boundaries for the ways that firms conduct business • Getting into the right industry, and then maneuvering for the right position within that industry • Strategies based on cost or differentiation		1980s

(continues)

Exhibit 3-1. (Continued).

Strategy	Unifying concept(s)	Talent history	Era
4. Competency strategies	• Strategy models directed inward on companies and their distinct core competencies/capabilities • Competitive advantage could be found in talent-based skills, collective learning, and the efforts of business leaders	• Productivity through people • Autonomy and entrepreneurship	1980s
5. Efficiency strategies	• Continuous assault on fixed costs • Push for operational efficiencies through quality, process reengineering • Businesses fundamentally reconfigured: leaner, flatter, cost-driven, process-organized	• Dismantling of long-term, reciprocal, employment model • Beginning of open talent market	1990s
6. Shorthand strategies	• Strategies rigid and inflexible—and inevitably outdated by the time they were produced • Substitutes for strategies sometimes in the form of a few key strategic processes and simple, easily communicated rules • Mechanisms for coping with an overload of opportunities	• Talent wars • Free agency	
7. Customer strategies	• Customer value propositions • Hands-on strategies developed and executed close to the customer	New talent perspectives	2000s

jobs, or classifications so painstakingly constructed by scientific management have much bearing on the way work is or will be organized, certainly in the United States.

Most work has a substantial knowledge component. And advanced knowledge is also a requirement for many *manual* operations in health care, computer systems, and broad categories of installation, maintenance, and repair. According to estimates from the Census Bureau, the number of workers using computers climbed from 24.2 million in 1984 to nearly 64 million in 1997, an average annual increase of 7.8 percent.[13] Clerks and workers have joined professionals and executives either as pure knowledge workers or as technologists (doing work that combines knowledge and manual work).[14] Talent is knowledge.

Knowledge workers and technologists have a level of work autonomy that once was reserved for executives and highly skilled professionals. Tasks used to program the worker.[15] Assembly line workers, for example, responded to the demands of a fragmented manufacturing process. Claims processors were programmed to respond to the arrival of forms. Now, because of the watershed impacts of competency and efficiency strategies, most programmable tasks have been reduced, eliminated, outsourced, or automated.

Instead of performing programmed tasks, knowledge-based talent is more likely to be responsible for either all or substantial portions of broader, considerably less supervised, considerably more value-added work processes. Individuals at all stages of their careers have considerable discretion to prioritize their time, efforts, and methods. As we have seen, these individuals are owners of human capital. Because of their unprecedented access to job knowledge, they become the resource best positioned to define and increase their own productivity. For that same reason, and probably also as never before, they need to know business strategy. The questions that drive the productivity of integrated knowledge work less often concern what precisely has to be done or precisely how to do it. Instead, questions concern why things are done and how they can be improved. And the source of the information is less often a supervisor and more often the knowledge worker.

Reality #2: Customers define talent's value

Customers have always paid talent's way. But customers do not necessarily value what talent provides; and they have seldom had direct control over it. The value provided by the Organization Man, for example, was mostly for internal organization exchange and consumption. This insulation of talent from customer value is changing in the era of customer strategies.

The most successful businesses have distinguished themselves by coming to terms with the important but unsettling reality that customers and markets do not care about companies and barely care about the products and services companies sell. In the customer seat (where, after all, we sit most of the time), products and services only have visibility and value if they improve customers' lives or contribute to customer success—that is, if they solve the problems that prompt customers to seek products and services in the first place.

Perhaps the first modern example of this realization was by IBM, which resulted in IBM's solution strategy approach. IBM's success during the 1950s did not grow from the quality and price competitiveness of its computers. Other computer manufacturers actually had more technologically advanced hardware, which performed better and at lower prices. What IBM pioneered was the profound understanding that its customers did not want computers; instead, they wanted solutions to business problems that happened to involve the storage, processing, and analysis of data. To that end IBM wrapped its hardware in solution products such as application software, and solution services such as installation, training, and maintenance that, when combined, provided complete business solutions.

This sort of "seeing it like it is" logic continues to contribute to the success of today's market leaders. Southwest Airlines, for example, describes itself—and then walks the talk—of not being an airline but instead being a customer service provider whose service happens to be air transportation (compare this with the in-the-box thinking that undid railroads in the nineteenth century).

The Container Store, a Dallas-based specialty retailer of home and office storage solutions, demonstrates talent value to customers through its substantial investment in new sales employee education. The retailer delivers 235 hours to new full-time employees during their first year, education that includes point of sale processes, sales skills, product knowledge, visual merchandising, and inventory management. By contrast, the norm for the retail industry is approximately seven hours annually.

And the experience of a Northeast-based financial services company illustrates how customer valuing of talent can be even more explicitly established and delivered. Determining through a survey what its insurance policy customers wanted most in terms of policy delivery time and accuracy, the company translated those customer values directly into employee performance requirements for contract delivery.

When you think about it, employers ultimately do not want employees. Instead, they want the correct and timely mix of talent who can either supply products/services customers value immediately or, longer term, do one or more of the following:

- Increase customer use and value perception of existing products/ services
- Develop or find new customers for existing products and services
- Develop new products/services that will be valued by existing customers and new customers

Making the connection between what customers value and what talent provides is a recurring new reality.

Reality #3: Talent is generational

While there have undoubtedly always been workplace-influencing generational differences—differences shaped by each generation's collective exposure to economic, historical, and political events—these differences have been accentuated by the acceleration and compaction of fundamental changes. The circumstances of the Organization Man workplace were stable for the greater part of two generations of U.S. talent. But the abrupt and paradigm-shifting events of the last twenty years have led to major differences in generational assumptions and expectations about work. These differences—especially those between the so-called baby boom and generation X generations—are captured in the research and writing of consulting firm Rainmaker Thinking and its founder Bruce Tulgan. According to Tulgan, there are now four distinct generations in the workforce. Older than baby boomers are what Tulgan terms the "silent generation" (those born before 1946). Younger than generation X is generation Y (those born after 1978). Each of these generations, argues Tulgan, has its own perspective on workplace relationships.[16]

Reality #4: Talent flow/engagement replaces employer commitment/employee loyalty

Both employers and talent now define their relationships in increasingly complex and contingent ways that have little to do with old employment models—but instead are usually influenced by the state of the market and factors such as the generational differences just described. Moreover, the state of the market is incredibly more complex: Both favorable and unfavorable markets stand side-by-side.

For example, even during the most heated days of the recent talent wars, layoffs occurred and even increased. Thirty-six percent of 1,441 companies surveyed by the American Management Association in its 2000 poll of hiring trends, reported engaging in simultaneous job creation and job elimination, up from 31 percent in 1996. The number of companies surveyed that reported eliminating jobs without creating any new positions was only 12.2 percent. About 30 percent of the companies also reported rehiring previously dismissed employees for new positions.

The goal of downsizing is now seldom only about achieving necessary cost cuts. Instead, it is about rearranging competencies. Because competencies belong to people not organizational systems, rearranging competencies means rearranging talent. Companies continue to hire while they downsize, shedding workers with obsolete skills and hiring new ones with skills in demand.[17] They are continually tailoring their workforces to fit the available work, adjusting quickly to swings in demand for products and services. Companies are striving to create a just-in-time workforce. And laid-off workers often, though reluctantly, agree with the business decisions that put them on the street.[18]

A Towers Perrin study conducted in the midst of the dot-com bust and the beginning of the broader technology slowdown—and published in the weeks immediately prior to the September 2001 terrorist attacks—showed, even in the growing shadow of massive layoffs, little let up in managers' continuing anxiety about finding talent.[19] According to the survey, 88 percent of company respondents believed that it was as difficult or even more difficult to recruit and retain talented employees. Also, 73 percent reported continuing to hire talented employees in the midst of downsizing, while 42 percent had created targeted programs to retain top performers. IBM Global Services division, where the success and growth over the past ten years have been impressive, currently employs one hundred fifty thousand people, up from a mere seventy-six hundred in 1992. Yet more than half of division employees have worked for the company for five years or less. In 1992, the figure was 14 percent.[20]

For their part, employees care about different things when joining a company than when they are deciding whether to stay or how much discretionary effort to give. More than ever talent shapes its views and contributions according to a variety of factors, among which the employer may be a diminishing part. When, for example, HR and business leaders look at employee attitude or morale surveys and are ready to congratulate themselves on attitude improvements, they might consider that these improvements may be more the function of a cooled employment marketplace than internal efforts and program initiatives. Similarly, employee handbooks with statements about the terms of the new employment relationship—for example, employee commitment to the company in exchange for company efforts to enhance the employability of its workers—reflect only the employer's version of the deal—their opening position—rather than the deal itself.

The new reality is a picture of a massively moving (or prepared to move) workforce in a contingent work world, a kaleidoscope of goings and comings that undercuts any accustomed sense of workplace commitment or continuity. At leadership levels—the organizational heights toward which Organization Man directed an entire career within the walls of one company—turnover is becoming the norm. In its 1999 "War for Talent" report based on a study of six thousand executives in seventy-seven corporations, management consulting firm McKinsey predicted that the average number of companies for which executives will work during a career will be 6.9—up from 5.2 today and 2.9 ten years ago.

Of course, one sizable segment of this contingent work world includes temporary workers: A forthcoming Census Bureau survey of three thousand companies finds that on a typical day these companies used temps and contract workers to meet 12 percent of their workforce needs, and, on peak days, their use reached 20 percent. Temps and contract workers currently account for nearly 5 percent of the U.S. workforce. In the United States, there are more than 33 million independent contractors and more people are employed by Manpower (the country's largest temporary agency) than by any *Fortune* 500 company. In fact, less than 10 percent of all employees work for a *Fortune* 500 company.

These circumstances have considerable meaning for the belonging to/working for distinction that began this chapter. The "belonging to" aspect has shifted dramatically away from companies and toward other competing allegiances: for example, professions, family, and lifestyle. It is considerably less realistic to view employment as a commitment— from either side of the transaction. Instead, the operative concept offered here is engagement: a reciprocal exchange of customer value (from talent) and career experience and skill enhancement value (from the employer) during a relatively brief but focused period of engagement

These circumstances also imply new meaning for the notion of "working for" an organization. This notion probably now means working for more companies than had previously been the case. But it also will mean—and does now—working for the same company in different roles at different times in different types of engagements—as employee, contractor, temporary or part-time, or consultant. This means a heightened importance to the notion of talent flow:

- Talent entering into a relationship with the company before employment
- Talent and company continuing and renewing the relationship around periods of engagement, both within traditional enterprise boundaries and across the looser boundaries of an extended enterprise

Notes

1. William H. Whyte, *The Organization Man* (New York: Doubleday, 1956), pp. 4, 130.

2. Ibid., p. 3.

3. Whyte was an academic sociologist who died in 1999. Among his other research work was a study of street life in an urban Italian-American neighborhood.

4. Whyte, p. 129.

5. To be distinguished from the post–World War II management science referred to in Chapter 2. Its originator, Frederick Winslow Taylor (1856–1915) first called his methods *task analysis* or *task management*.

6. Combinations of motions, effort, and time stripped of waste, optimized, and recombined into jobs.

7. Peter F. Drucker, *Management Challenges for the 21st Century* (New York: HarperBusiness, 1999), p. 136.

8. Peter Cappelli, *The New Deal at Work* (Boston: Harvard Business School Press, 1999), p. 4

9. Ibid. p. 5.

10. Ibid., p. 9.

11. Not lost in this was the reality that coordination, communication, and intermediation skills were also the competencies that defined the HR function and HR practitioners. Under the new market arrangements—with initially slack-

ened hiring demand and with the employer-employee relationship balance shifted dramatically to the advantage of the employer—some critics questioned the very need for a distinct HR function.

12. Cappelli, p. 99

13. Robert Kominski and Eric Newburger, "Access Denied: Changes in Computer Ownership and Use: 1984–1997," August 1999. (www.census.gov/ population/www/socdemo/computer.html)

14. Drucker, p. 149.

15. Ibid., p. 144.

16. Bruce Tulgan, *Winning the Talent Wars*, Eighty-Third Edition, February 19, 2002 (online newsletter at www.rainmakerthinking.com).

17. Cappelli, p. 6.

18. Louis Uchitelle, "As Job Cuts Spread, Tears Replace Anger," *The New York Times*, August 5, 2001, section 3, p. 1 (Business p. 1).

19. *The Towers Perrin Talent Report: New Realities in Today's Workforce.* The study was conducted in the United States and Canada during April and May of 2001. A total of 5,707 randomly selected employees from companies with more than five hundred employees responded. Of those, 4,942 were from the United States, and 765 were from Canada. Three-quarters of the respondents were from *Fortune* 1000 companies. Nearly 30 percent of the respondents were managers.

20. Steve Lohr, "He Loves to Win. At IBM, He Did," *The New York Times*, March 10, 2002, p. B11.

PART II

Building, Delivering, and Measuring Talent Strategies

CHAPTER 4

☑ TALENT STRATEGIES: SCANNING

I N THIS CHAPTER, LET US assume that talent strategies are owned and orchestrated by HR, while leaving room for other possible arrangements For example:

- Talent strategies may be incorporated into core business strategy planning.
- Talent strategies may be decentralized to the SBU or department level with HR in a business partner role.

Whatever the arrangement, our belief is that talent strategies should have company-level impact.

After defining talent strategies, we will preview the overall process of evaluating, selecting, implementing, and measuring strategy initiatives. The balance of this chapter will concentrate on the first of these stages: evaluating strategy alternatives. Choosing strategy initiatives, strategy delivery, and strategy measurement will be separate topics in succeeding chapters.

Talent strategies management cycle

A business's talent strategies are both plans and patterns of behavior for creating and sustaining advantages in markets where it competes to recruit, retain, motivate, and reward the performance of key talent. Talent strategies establish the match between what a company is capable of doing to meet business talent needs within the universe of what it might do given the constraints and opportunities in the employment marketplace. (See Exhibit 4-1.)

What concerns us here is the formation of a broader talent strategies approach. Thinking, prioritizing, and acting within this broader framework is lacking when HR tangles itself in reaction and administrative myopia; when, to adapt Drucker's words, HR is a function that does not deal with talent and is not strategic. Essential strategy questions are:

- Where are we going?
- What do we have to do to get there?
- And who will be responsible for execution?

These questions are often preempted in favor of tactical how-to questions. For many organizations, the war for talent has been waged amidst confusion and reaction. In the war ahead, strategy should play a more central role.

Business strategies

Talent strategies start with understanding business strategies, as discussed in Chapter 2. Business strategies are, after all, the atmosphere in

Exhibit 4-1. Talent strategies management cycle.

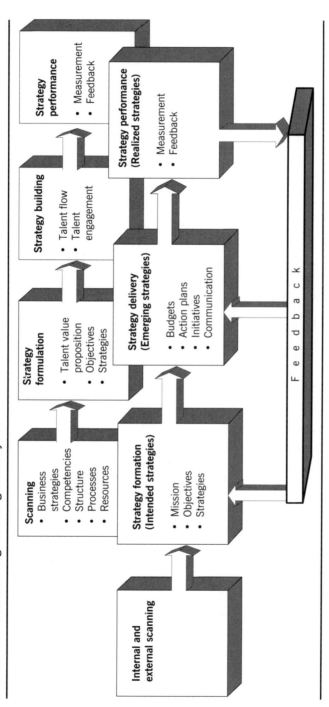

which talent strategies breathe. Business strategies—long term by way of the business strategy management cycle; short term through a combination of the top-down strategy plan, bottom-up action plans, and budgets—ultimately plug into fundamental talent strategies, initiatives, and processes:

- The competencies and quantity of talent to be recruited, deployed, and retained to drive business strategies determine the relating, recruiting, and retaining components of what we call here talent flow strategies.
- The talent requirements that are missing in the current workforce, but that cannot be met through recruiting, determine the learning components of what we call here talent engagement strategies.
- The company's strategic market, customer, and competitor positioning determine the rewards component of talent engagement strategies. For example, the choice to be in a particular industry means that pay for key talent will be heavily influenced by industry pay market trends. Similarly, the need to compete on price will heavily impact pay practices; for example, the use of alternative, noncash rewards and the time horizon of pay arrangements.
- Finally, business strategies directly influence the priorities of work initiatives, the focus of performance, and the specific types of talent behaviors (for example, in customer relationships) most likely to contribute to strategy success. In this sense, business strategies determine the performance management component of talent engagement strategies.

From HR's vantage "getting" the business strategy definition means thinking, questioning, and translating business strategies into talent issues, needs, objectives, and strategy initiatives for meeting those objectives. Human resources should have an eye toward so-called human capital obstacles in the way of successfully accomplishing strategic initiatives. The sources of this information are its internal customers:

business unit- and department-level executives. It means asking questions such as:

- What are the business's strategic objectives and how are these objectives translated into business unit or department objectives?
- What do unit managers feel are the key obstacles and drivers of those objectives?
- How do the talent skills, motivation, and workforce structure impact key drivers?
- How can talent flow and talent engagement strategies, tools, and processes influence the skills, motivation, and workforce structure to remove obstacles and fuel drivers?

The answers to these questions ultimately determine the content of talent strategies. But a necessary concurrent step is to grapple with these questions against the reality backdrop of conditions both inside and outside the company. In other words, talent strategy builders need to objectively scan and assess:

- Internal strengths and weaknesses related to the competencies, structure, processes, and current talent stock of the company
- External opportunities and threats presented by the markets for talent

Internal scanning: competencies

A company's competencies are its people-embodied assets—the skills, capabilities, and information that talent and, therefore, the organization possesses. Distinctive competencies are further defined in terms of customer-perceived benefits. They are not only the organization's best skills and capabilities but also the skills and capabilities that enable it to compete on factors other companies do poorly or not at all. They leverage a company's ability to succeed in new markets, to be a leader in generating new products, or to satisfy new customer categories.[1]

It is important to distinguish what is a short list (typically numbering from five to fifteen) of *business-level* competencies from the detailed competencies used to describe or define jobs, departments, functions, and work processes. These *work level* competencies can be looked at as the trees that populate the forests of business-level competencies. (Work-level competencies are discussed in Chapter 6.) Business-level competencies provide the context for work-level competencies.

Distinctive business-level competencies provide a particular benefit that is recognized by customers.[2] When a company is described as having a market-oriented or product-oriented or technology-oriented culture, these descriptions are really about the distinctive competencies that are projected to customers. For example:

- Among Sony Corporation's core business-level competencies are its distinctive capabilities to innovate and miniaturize in consumer electronics—competencies where the historical roots trace to a three-hundred-year-old tradition of artistic miniaturization.[3]
- IBM's core competencies combine its ability to provide integrated solutions—distilling the complexity of computing to solve a client's business problems—with its research prowess.
- A core competency unique to Wal-Mart and Federal Express, each in a different industry, is logistics management. For example, Wal-Mart's strategy of removing boundaries between itself and key vendors, allowing vendors to stock products directly on store shelves and allowing Wal-Mart to sharply reduce warehoused inventories, enable Wal-Mart to strip away one third of its operating costs.
- For Southwest Airlines, in transportation, its business-level competencies include customer service innovations and industry-leading capabilities in flight scheduling.
- For Cisco Systems, three core business-level strategic competencies are its cutting-edge network hardware design capabilities, its

customer relationship skills, and its practiced expertise in acquiring and integrating small technology businesses.

These business-level competencies transcend particular products and services; they serve as channels for a broadening array of new products and services. They are not legacies of the past such as brand names or an installed customer base; instead, they are skills directed toward future competition.

These competencies should be identified not only in terms of what the organization has now but also in terms of what it will need in the future. Identifying a few strategy-level competencies provides a clear framework. Current and future competency gaps provide the basis for defining talent strategies objectives. In other words, what competencies are missing or declining? Which need to be deepened, developed, or acquired?

Internal scanning: structure

Organizational structure—the company's pattern of communication, authority, and work process flow relationships—should follow business strategies. If structure is compatible with strategy, then structure is an asset. If not—if, for example, a centralized organization's strategy is to launch international operations better suited to a decentralized divisional structure—then structure is a weakness. Poor fits can cripple or doom strategies.

Despite the organization compression and streamlining that have occurred over the past twenty years; despite periodic rebellions against the very notion of hierarchies, formal structures, and organization charts; and despite the infinite combinations of structures that can be— and are being—devised, some basic organizational structures remain in wide use.[4] We summarize five structures here (see Exhibit 4-2), the first three depicting the succession of structures that companies go through as they form, grow, and expand; the last two reflecting more specialized organization settings and structures.

Exhibit 4-2. Structures, business strategies, and talent.

Simple structure
-No formal function or product/service categories
-Small, entrepreneurial company
-Market niche
-Cross-functional, collegial talent

Functional structure
-Medium-size company with several product/service lines
-Functional talent specialists

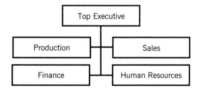

Divisional structure
-Large company
-Many product/service lines in related industries
-Talent functional specialties according to product/service/market differences
-Cross-division functional talent links

Special: Project/product/process matrix structure
-May begin as temporary cross-functional task forces
-May then evolve into product/service brand management with function as primary organization relationships
-May eventually evolve into true matrix with dual function and product/service relationships

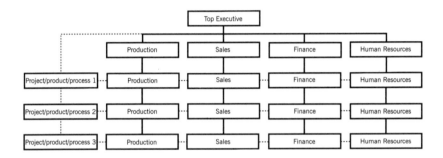

Virtually integrated structure
-Networked organization of divisions, subsidiaries, contractors

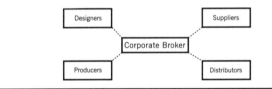

Just as each organization structure has a bearing on strategy and products or services, each organization also has implications for talent strategies. Among the implications are:

- Will talent competencies be oriented around functional professions (more likely in a functional or divisional structure) or multi-function process-oriented skills (more likely in a simple or matrix structure)?
- How will talent strategies and initiatives be delivered: for example, from corporate level; at SBU or divisional levels; or through a combination of levels?

- What will be the mix of traditional (full-time, on-site, exclusive) and nontraditional (contractor, project-dependent) talent employment?
- Will talent growth and development opportunities be centered on projects (matrix structure) or on roles in divisional or functional settings?
- What are the logical points of entry for new and experienced talent?
- What are possible barriers for talent deployment?
- If there is a poor fit between strategy and structure, what will be the talent implications of realigning organization structure to better suit strategy?

Internal scanning: talent processes

The competitive pressures of global markets, the need to deliver higher shareholder value, the relentless drive to reduce fixed costs—the business realities described in Chapter 2—made at least the phrase process reengineering familiar to nearly everyone in the business world, and eventually a source of anxiety and job insecurity to many. During the economic downturn of the early to mid-1990s, it seemed that business leaders tried to associate every belt-tightening activity with the Darwinian inevitability of reengineering.

Reengineering, the term introduced, or at least put on the map, by Michael Hammer and James Champy in their bestseller *Reengineering the Corporation,* became the shorthand reason (or the excuse) for the rounds of reorganization, restructuring, delayering, rightsizing, and job losses that followed.[5] And of course, reengineering also became synonymous with employer abandonment of the traditional model of lifetime employment.

Reengineering involved the demolition of bureaucratic and previously market-immune internal administrative functions. It followed from fundamental rethinking—by looking outward to the customer rather than inward at the organization or upward to the boss. It then led to fundamental questions: Why do we have this function? Why are we doing this transaction? How does this meet customer needs?

In truth, many companies limited their reengineering efforts to demolition and the cutting of jobs and other expenses. What often went undone was the less dramatic but ultimately more productive work of redesigning and simplifying dysfunctional activities in manufacturing, sales, finance, human resources, and other functions. When done correctly, this work created streamlined end-to-end business processes that provided real customer value as well as considerable expense reduction.

Hammer and Champy originally defined a business process as "a collection of activities that takes one or more kinds of input and creates an output that is of value to the customer."[6] More recently, Hammer fine-tuned the business process concept to "an organized group of related activities that together create a result of value to the customers."[7]

Under either definition, business processes are broader and more strategic in nature than business transactions. Business processes combine and coordinate transactions; cut across barriers of departments, time constraints, and bureaucracy; and are focused more on the needs of the customer and less on those of the processor—or his supervisor.

But business processes have upper and lower boundaries. Built too large or trying to cover too much, processes become unmanageable behemoths that frustrate coordination and defy execution. Cut too fine, they lapse into transactions that may be pleasing to the processor but lack a customer. There are many separate transactions involved in recruiting, screening, and hiring talent. While most of the intervening transactions may be essential, the real value for the customers—the hiring manager, the talent prospect—arrives when the person starts. The customer is not as concerned with the intervening steps as with the quality and timeliness of the outcome.

HR often lacks a process reputation, or, if it has one, mysteries, obstacles, and delays often characterize the processes. If HR is organized rigidly and silolike into disciplines such as staffing, compensation, benefits, and employee relations, its services may have the look and feel of silos within silos. (See Exhibit 4-3.) Exhibit 4-4 depicts departmental

Exhibit 4-3. Silos within silos.

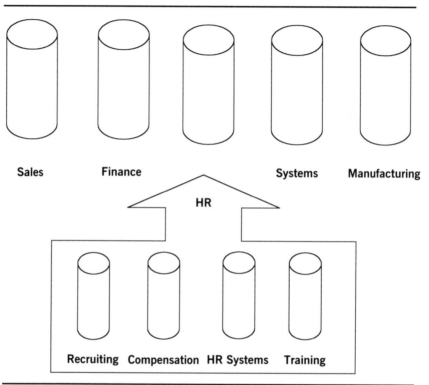

functions realigned to processes. The difference, much more than semantic, is organizing work both across the HR department and across
the range of other business functions. Some of the keys are:

- Being able to cut across organizational barriers to deliver speed
  and efficiency, while avoiding fragmented results
- Organizing either teams or individuals to accomplish complex
  processes provided they receive sufficient discretion and end-to-
  end process authority
- Recognizing that since the idea is to deliver customer value, the
  customer in essence "supervises" the process and should be able
  to establish the meaning of *value*

Exhibit 4-4. Talent process orientation.

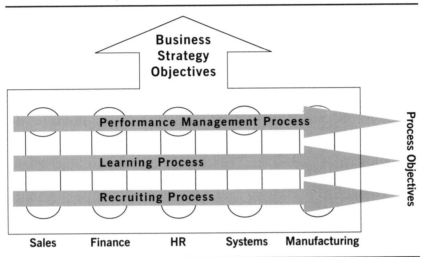

What is important about processes in the current context is getting a sense of how strategy-ready are the company's repertoire of processes for managing what we introduced in Chapter 1 as talent flow (people at the right time with the needed competencies) and talent engagement (prepared, motivated, and rewarded for strategy-based achievement). One issue here is determining the number, purpose, and demarcations of these processes. This will vary by organization, the volume of talent transactions, and the resources available to accomplish them. For our current purpose, we will identify six processes around which talent strategy initiatives can be built. We will group them under *talent flow* and *talent engagement* (and depicted in Exhibit 4-5) as follows:

TALENT FLOW:

- *Relating*—Prerecruitment process for identifying key talent and establishing relationships; postemployment process for maintaining relationships
- *Recruiting*—Talent acquisition process
- *Retaining*—Processes designed to extend the talent engagement cycle

Exhibit 4-5. Strategic talent processes.

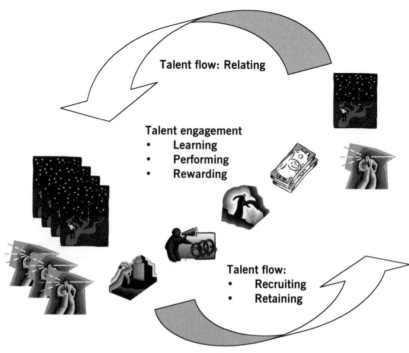

TALENT ENGAGEMENT:

- *Performance management* processes—For providing feedback and direction on work performance
- *Learning*—Competency and performance-based learning
- *Rewarding*—Monetary and nonmonetary rewards that reinforce customer-focused performance as well as defining the talent/employment value exchange

Six processes is a hefty number and might reasonably be combined. Looking at the business as a whole, the six might more accurately be described as subprocesses under an overall human resources process. Nevertheless, we suggest sticking with something like this list to assess, process by process, going into talent strategy-building, the organization's strengths, weaknesses, and gaps when it comes to executing processes. An evaluation tool can be used similar to the one shown in Exhibit 4-6, which stacks the processes against successful reengineering criteria adapted from Hammer and Champy's work. Quite simply, fewer Xs usually means more fragmentation and less process-orientation. More importantly, and not so simply, this is a juncture for judging the strategic value of talent processes. In the context of business strategy directions, core competencies, and the quality and depth of current talent resources, which of the processes:

- Are most critical to business strategies?
- Need to be distinctive (or at sustained or maintenance level)?
- Warrant the most attention?
- Should be delivered internally?
- Should be considered for outsourcing, in whole or in part?
- Can provide the basis for talent strategy initiatives that best support business strategies?

Two other points about talent processes: First, in addition to revamping HR transactions into value-delivering processes, HR can facilitate—or at least not block—the progress of processes in other parts of the business. One obstacle to remove may be the often-outmoded use of jobs and salary grades as the organizing concepts for work performance and pay. In many business environments, the organizing principle of self-contained jobs has either shifted, or is in the process of shifting to the organizing principle of integrated work processes and competencies.

Second, process orientation is usually easier in smaller companies and in smaller HR groups, in any setting really, where, from a resource standpoint, strict functional groupings are less feasible. That is not to say that potential infighting is any less intense or siloing is any more porous because the arena is smaller.

Internal scanning: talent resources

GE's annual human resources review probably sets the gold standard for ongoing internal scanning of key talent resources with its annual

Exhibit 4-6. Scanning and evaluating current talent processes.

	1. Several jobs are combined into one: processes and responsibilities are compressed to reduce processes and administrative overhead	2. Workers make decisions: decisionmaking is part of the real work	3. Process steps performed in natural order: work is sequenced in terms of what needs to follow what; no stopping and waiting for others to finish their piece; enough information is exchanged to keep process moving
Rewarding			
Performing			
Learning			
Talent engagement			
Retaining			
Recruiting			
Relating			
Talent flow			

4. **Multiple version processes:** triage approach; routine situations—get handled one way; special situations channeled to separate process version						
5. **Work is performed where it makes most sense:** work shifts across organizational boundaries to improve process performance						
6. **Checks and controls are reduced:** sometimes aggregated, sometimes deferred (like spending limits on credit cards)						
7. **Reconciliation is minimized:** reduces contact points where inconsistencies have to be reconciled						
8. **Use of "case manager":** expediter of complex processes						
9. **Balanced use of centralization and decentralization**						

See Michael Hammer and James Champy, *Reengineering the Corporation* (New York: HarperBusiness, 1994), pp. 51–63.

Session C meetings—a talent management process that actually predates Jack Welch's tenure as CEO. Annually in April and May, each of GE's twelve businesses convene for full-day Session C meetings to personally review the performance and developmental plans for GE's top three thousand managers. Session C reviews typically involve fourteen-hour days, with each session conducted by the business's CEO and senior human-resources executive. For each employee under review there is a briefing book containing the employee's self-assessment of strengths and weaknesses, developmental needs, and short- and long-term goals. Also included is their supervisor's analysis.[8]

The Session C review format forces those running the units to identify future leaders, make bets on early-career "stretch" assignments, develop succession plans for all key jobs, and decide which high-potential executives should be sent to leadership training. Session C reviews give GE's SBU managers a broad, comparative view of their teams; and by reviewing the groups annually, they are also able to assess talent in the context of ongoing strategies.

GE's thirty or more years of experience with Session C contrasts mightily with the degree of internal talent scanning performed by most companies. In our experience and research, few companies have meaningful or reliable information about the quality and capacity of their current talent resources. For example, only 16 percent of senior executives surveyed in McKinsey's "War for Talent" studies indicated that their companies actually knew who were the high and low performers.[9] Although many companies go through the motions of talent reviews or succession planning, they tend to do so intermittently, with limited rigor, and with little ambition to go deeply into the organization segment under review. Most lack evidence and a vocabulary for expressing the readiness of their talent to accomplish business strategies.

This is a crucial issue because there is both logic and evidence to suggest that business strategy deliberations should begin not with "what" or "where"—the strategic model, vision, or destination—but with "who"—the ability and capacity of key players responsible for strategy delivery whatever its content or destination. When, for example, David Maxwell took the helm as CEO of a financially crippled Fannie Mae in 1981, his first strategic priority was to interview and assess his twenty-six-person executive team (fourteen of whom were subsequently replaced) to get the "right people on the bus, the wrong people off the bus, and the right people in the right seats."[10]

For companies without the track record like GE or the turnaround urgency of Fannie Mae, internal talent assessment should begin with a clean and straightforward mechanism to evaluate competencies against the business's strategy objectives. Key points here are to:

- Avoid mechanisms that get bogged down in details over definitions, comprehensive skill sets, or action plans—that is, putting more effort into finding out "who is on the bus" instead of the bus's destination or progress
- Focus on mechanisms that provide concise snapshots that can be clarified or fleshed out through individual interviews or focus groups
- Establish mechanisms and systems that can be refined and reused (for example, as follow-up snapshots) as strategies are developed and delivered

Exhibit 4-7 presents one example of a tool that can be adapted for summarizing assessments by company leaders about the readiness of current talent to deliver on strategy objectives. The tool provides a framework for obtaining an initial assessment of talent readiness against strategic objectives, competencies, or both.

Obviously there can be a great deal of flexibility in the process for capturing and coding the information. One option is to identify the percentage of talent in each level of readiness across each talent category. Information for each level of readiness—especially where competency readiness falls short—can be coded for the reasons that are most prevalent or anticipated. Where all competencies may not be pertinent to all talent levels, portions of the data collection tool can be coded as *not*

Exhibit 4-7. Talent readiness assessment.

# Business strategy objective ##. Strategy related competency	Leadership talent			Knowledge talent			Technologist talent		
	Falls short	Meets	Exceeds	Falls short	Meets	Exceeds	Falls short	Meets	Exceeds
1									
1.1	% (= 100% across talent category), reason codes (letter codes or both)								
1.2									
1.3									
2									
2.1									
2.2									
2.3									
3									
3.1									
3.2									
3.3									

Reason codes:

a.
b.
c.
d.
e.

applicable; alternatively, competency descriptions can be provided that distinguish the competency as it applies to each talent category.

It is crucially important to distinguish this type of tool from efforts to survey head-count needs or recruiting plans. That sort of assessment most often occurs as a function of the budgeting process—although head-count data from budgeting may also provide important information about competency gaps.

An additional perspective on internal talent resources comes from doing a generational scan. Recall from Chapter 3 that there are currently four generations in the workforce, each distinguished to a certain extent by its own work/life experiences. Sorting the company's talent into a matrix of talent and generation categories—while exercising caution both about the use or dissemination of individual information on age; and about treating generational status as the only controlling influence on work expectations, preferences, and behaviors—can provide useful insights into a range of talent/strategy issues, such as:

- The leadership style and expectations of those responsible for business strategy formation—are they predominantly Silents? Boomers? Gen Xers?
- The most effective leadership and communication styles for strategy delivery
- Receptivity to strategies involving significant change, especially in structure
- The amount, content, and delivery method of learning resources that will need to accompany strategy delivery
- Talent relationships where there are significant generation gaps (for example, between Silents and Gen X/Gen Y) leading to potential conflicts or disruptions in leadership, performance management, or communication; or, alternatively, creating situations where coaching and mentoring should be strongly encouraged

External scanning: current and projected markets for talent

The final scanning target is, of course, the talent marketplace. As in business strategies, talent strategies have customers and competitors. The customer in this case is the talent essential to core competency needs, the competitors are the range and attractiveness of other employment alternatives.

The issue underlying this evaluation is whether enough of the right talent can be acquired to accomplish business objectives. Assuming an infinite supply of the right workers at the right price is a risky but all too common component of business strategies. It is important to understand the sometimes-discouraging limitations of the talent market.

Although it is important to understand the traditional job seeker talent market, it is also important to consider broadening the definition of the market to include a wide range of talent resources, including independent contractors, temps, consultants, part-timers, flex-timers, telecommuters, outside companies, former employees, and even previous job applicants who've declined offers.

The most resonant real-world example of this concept of talent reserves is the U.S. military. Each of the services has a full-time active duty component supplemented by a Federal Reserve component. In addition, each state, district, and territory has organized Army and Air National Guard units. Compared with the cost of maintaining a large standing military force, the Reserves are a cost-effective way to maintain a large accessible force of trained and equipped talent. During 2000, for example, reserve forces provided nearly 12.1 million person-days of military service—the equivalent of adding thirty-three thousand full-time personnel to the active force.

External scanning: where now?

Not that long ago, and certainly throughout the long era of Organization Man, employers assessed the external talent market—if they felt they needed to—at a leisurely, almost glacial pace. Things did not change drastically, employment marketplaces were predominantly internal marketplaces, and employers largely held the information cards. But, as we suggested in Chapter 1, the situation has changed with the advent of the new employment marketplace.

On the surface, the transparency of this marketplace—the explosion of online job-posting sites; ocean-size data-based résumé repositories; the requisite careers link on virtually all company Web sites; the vast and seemingly equalizing stores of information about pay rates and employment circumstances—would seem to create leverage for talent sellers and a frictionless communications outlet of employers. In truth, the marketplace, for all the advances it offers in communications reach and transaction speed, can be a considerable source of frustration and diminishing returns for both parties at the part of the economic cycle where each could benefit most from the marketplace.

In the case of talent sellers in an economic downturn, the marketplace only seems to offer more places to search where no jobs can be found. Conversely, for employment buyers in a talent seller's market, the marketplace often seems to provide a vast landscape of dry wells.

We will discuss this point more fully when we consider talent flow strategies. For now, and to conclude our discussion of the scanning stage, let us touch on the implications for talent strategies scanning. The essence of a customer and competitor scan might once have boiled down to: "Where got, where go?" In other words, where does our talent come from? And when they leave us, where do they go? These continue to be valid and essential market-scanning questions. But a third question should be added to the mix, and certainly for the talent needed to sustain and advance the company's distinctive competencies: "Where now?" In other words, where are people with whom we need to initiate and cultivate relationships? Identifying these people and entering into a relationship with them is a new and indispensable environment-scanning priority. It is a scanning activity best done when these people are needed least—but are the most visible; it is an activity whose rewards will be evident when their talent is needed most.

Few businesses maintain realistic assessments of their market and possible talent reserves—although many individual managers do so, at least on an informal basis, in the interests of handling inevitable fluctuations in talent needs and availability. Many organizations have, however, begun to realize that talent relationship building can be a valuable talent strategy initiative.

Capturing internal/external scans

At this stage it might be easy to become frustrated by how little is really known about talent capabilities either inside, outside, or at the boundaries of the company. This reality usually stands in sharp contrast to the numerous and quite detailed data points about physical and financial assets. The frustration is understandable, but it should be balanced with the equally important reality that you don't need to have all the answers or get everything right up front. The idea instead is to capture what important intelligence you can at the start and use that as the basis for additional intelligence gathering as talent strategy initiatives are chosen, formed, delivered, measured, and improved.

With this in mind, an important step is to filter and condense information from the internal and external scans into a preliminary assessment of talent strengths and weaknesses (internal), and opportunities and threats (external) that can be used (and periodically updated) as the basis for setting talent strategy priorities and objectives. A basic example of this type of assessment is shown in Exhibit 4-8. Depending on the quality and reliability of scanning data, this combined internal/external assessment can be limited to qualitative information or quantified with weights, ratings, and weighted scores.

Exhibit 4-8. Internal/external scanning summary.

Internal factors	Weight (Factor importance)	Rating	Weighted score	Comments
Strengths:				
• Strong retention rates during first year of employment	.05	3	.15	• Workforce stability • Evidence of career growth
• Several key internal promotions viewed favorably by staff	.05	3	.15	
• Solid results from staff survey of product knowledge, strategy understanding	.15	4	.6	• People on same strategy page
• "Intrapreneurial" program initiative generating enthusiastic response	.05	3	.15	• Reinforcing entrepreneur mindset
Weaknesses:				
• New sales staff lacks significant industry experience	.075	2	.15	• Need focus on track record hires
• CFO departure	.05	1	.05	• Uneasiness among finance staff
• Pay benchmark	.1	2	.2	• Lagging pay in key areas
• Early retirement departures expected in key operations roles	.05	2	.1	• Replacement strategies not in place

(continues)

Exhibit 4-8. (Continued).

External factors	Weight (Factor importance)	Rating	Weighted score	Comments
Opportunities:				
• Recent downsizing by competitor XYZ	.05	3	.15	• May result in sales staff defections
• Favorable press about recent product release successes	.15	4	.6	• Solidifying perception stability, industry leader
• MBA campus recruiting program in 3rd year	.05	4	.2	• Yielding results
Threats:				
• Key technology leaders being contacted by search firms	.05	2	.1	• Threat of talent loss
• Major highway construction project projected for 2 years; worsens commute	.025	1	.025	• Possible recruiting/turnover factor
• New product releases giving technology and product management staff visibility	.1	4	.4	• Exposure to competing employment opportunities
Total weighted score	1.00		3.03	

Process

- Identify important internal strengths and weaknesses; external opportunities and threats; in the comments column indicate why factor was chosen/what its impact will be.
- Apply weight to each S.W.O.T.; combined total must = 1.0
- Rate each factor based on the organization's response to the factor 1 = poor, 2 = below average, 3 = average, 4 = above average, 5 = outstanding
- Total the weighted scores; 5 = outstanding, 3 = average, 1 = poor

Notes

1. Gary Hamel and C.K. Prahalad, *Competing for the Future* (Boston: Harvard Business School Press, 2001), p. 242.

2. Ibid., 219.

3. Peter F. Drucker, "The Information Executives Truly Need" in *Harvard Business Review on Measuring Corporate Performance* (Boston: Harvard Business School Press, 1998), p. 15.

4. One of Louis Gerstner's first actions when he assumed leadership at IBM in 1993 was to abolish the ritual of IBM organization charts. When asked how to revise the organization under his management, he declared that it wouldn't be through organization charts and that anyone asking for one was focusing on the wrong thing.

5. Michael Hammer and James Champy, *Reengineering the Corporation* (New York: HarperBusiness, 1994).

6. Ibid., p. 35.

7. Michael Hammer, *Agenda* (New York: Crown Business, 2001), p. 53.

8. "How Welch Manages GE," *Business Week*, June 6, 1998, p. 105.

9. Ed Michaels, Helen Handfield-Jones, and Beth Axelrod, *The War for Talent* (Boston: Harvard Business School Press, 2001), pp. 14–15.

10. Jim Collins, "Good to Great," *Fast Company*, October 2001, pp. 90–95.

CHAPTER 5

☑ TALENT STRATEGY BUILDING

THROUGHOUT THE TALENT WARS, EMPLOYERS were bombarded with advice, some of it contradictory, impractical, or all too obvious, but much of it sound, on how to recruit and retain key talent as the talent marketplace kicked into overdrive. Much of this advice was presented in pragmatic, well-reasoned, feasible "to-do" lists. The challenge of such lists—and a challenge faced in this book, as well—is that they risk being transplanted into business settings to compete against numerous influences, priorities, and resource constraints. These lists are often embraced by one person or only a handful of people, when many of the recommendations are matters intended (at least initially) for the agendas of organizations rather than the individual to-do lists of managers. Unfortunately, because even the best sets of principles cannot be applied all at once, they often end up not being applied at all.

That is where strategies come in. One value of a purposeful strategy building process is to stage and filter laundry lists of best practices into initiatives that make sense in settings (that is, the company's business culture) and sequences that also make sense. Company culture can be a potent driver or an insurmountable obstacle. Strategies integrate promising ideas, approaches, and initiatives into the context of a company so that, depending on the need, culture can be mobilized or culture can begin to change.

The authors of *The War for Talent* conclude that the right leadership mind-set—"the fundamental belief in the value of talent"[1]—rather than specific processes makes the biggest difference in talent strategy success. But that mind-set, if it is indeed underdeveloped, won't result from a flash of enlightenment. It is actually a strategic change issue, and in the following three senses:

1. It is strategic to identify (by measurement rather than conjecture) whether the talent mind-set is a priority that will make or break business strategy objectives.
2. Building the mind-set involves strategy initiatives—communication and business case building, to begin with—more than exasperation or exhortation.
3. Even when a talent mind-set holds sway, strategies and processes must still deliver the features that the mind-set makes doable. "Weaving development" into the organization, for example, or "paying for performance, and nothing else" are possible strategy objectives. They don't materialize and they are not inevitable, instead they happen through a sequence of planning, resource allocation, process, policy, and action.

Talent strategy components

Business strategy building—again, stripping away the infinite configurations of players and procedures that companies use—involves four basic components:

1. *Mission.* A concept statement that distills business intentions, beliefs, and values and links them to an idealistic but achievable business future. Mission statements are public narratives—part vision, part mantra, and part strategy plan.
2. *Objectives.* The quantifiable end results of planned strategic activities: what is to be accomplished, by whom, and when.
3. *Strategy initiatives.* How, through plans and actions, the company will live up to its mission and reach its objectives.
4. *Policies and processes.* Ground rules and instruction sets for strategy delivery and decision making. When business strategies are formed at a corporate level, these are guidelines for division or functional strategies. The GE edict to its twelve major businesses to be number one or number two where they choose to compete is a prime example. Policies and processes, then, are strategies dispersed through the organization for execution.

With several variations in terminology, perspective, and emphasis, talent strategies build on similar components: One is that talent strategies substitute talent value propositions for mission statements. Second is the added importance of process, a topic explored in Chapter 4. Even after more than a decade of process engineering, talent processes remain, at least in many of the organizations we see, fragmented and widely dispersed. Dispersion is not the problem, but resulting inconsistency and process ownership issues are. Talent is often treated as a team, department, or even manager asset, instead of as an organization asset. When it comes to talent strategies and strategy objectives, there is often low-hanging fruit to be picked through talent process prioritizing, streamlining, improvement, and execution. Third is the talent ingredient itself in talent strategies. As we anticipate the strategy processes and initiatives profiled in Chapters 6 and 7, we'll touch on the important role of strategy athletes in making successful talent-based strategies happen.

Talent value propositions

A crucial juncture in business strategy formation—and a juncture where many strategies stumble—occurs when leaders and business strategists attempt to move visions and strategic intentions from complexity toward simplification and delivery by way of mission statements. Most businesses are ultimately able to hone broad concepts into succinct statements, although the process may often become bogged down in introspection and foot-dragging.

Sometimes mission determination bypasses methodical discussion and collaboration. When, for example, IBM chairperson and CEO Louis Gerstner initially disdained IBM's need for a strategic vision, it was because of his concern that a debate over vision might drag on endlessly while the company foundered. Within six months—and largely based on Gerstner's interactions with IBM customers—an ultimately successful vision/mission to rebuild IBM "from the customer back, not from the company out" emerged.

Mission statements are for public consumption, although they often have as much or more meaning inside the organization. Mission statements are intended to inform and guide, but also to inspire. They serve different purposes at different junctures in an organization's life. For example, the mission statement may be designed by a company to mobilize against a competitive opponent or it may be aimed, as in IBM's case, at internal transformation.

Good mission statements are direct, vivid, and distinctive to the companies that create them—and they are not always called *mission statements*. Not surprisingly, statements are frequently cast in terms of customer value. Customer value propositions define how the business distinguishes itself from competitors to attract, retain, and deepen relations with targeted customers. The value proposition also has an internal as well as an external impact: It helps the organization to prioritize and direct its internal processes toward improved customer outcomes. Smart businesses center their value propositions on distinguishing competencies—it might be operations, for example, or product quality or customer relationships—an area where they can excel in the customers' eyes while maintaining threshold standards in others.[2] If the value proposition involves customer service and scheduling, as it does with Southwest Airlines, then resource bets are well placed on customer services processes and technologies. If the value proposition involves logistics, as is the case with Federal Express, then logistic processes rightly have center stage.

The impact of customer value propositions is that they both challenge and sell. (Of course, a customer value proposition ultimately works only if its products/services are as compelling as the statements that represent them.) Some examples of mission and customer value propositions from among *Fortune* magazine's 2002 list of America's Most Admired Companies are shown in Exhibit 5-1. (See the discussion later in this chapter in the section titled Employer of Choice and in the notes that conclude this chapter for information on talent-targeted best employer lists.)

Talent strategists should similarly define customer value propositions, this time in the form of talent value propositions. Determining solid talent value propositions is among the first orders of business in talent strategy building because it helps to identify your business in the employment marketplace. An effective talent value proposition can be used as a persuasive tool, both internally and externally, for sourcing, recruiting, and retaining talent.

Good talent value propositions are built around employment factors that differentiate and distinguish companies as employers. As with good customer value propositions, good talent value propositions play to real strengths rather than inventing imaginary advantages. Good talent value propositions are also consistent with customer value propositions. Why? Because customers and talent prospects do not live in different worlds. A company cannot be one thing to its consumer audience, yet expect to be another to talent prospects, because they are often one and the same. After all, one in five people who apply for work at a particular company do so because of that company's product market advertisements. Sports merchandiser Nike's "just do it" slogan, for example, has proved to be a value proposition not only to consumers but also to current and prospective employees. Similarly, Patagonia, a 570-employee, Reno, Nevada–based "environmentally conscious maker of quality outdoor clothing" specifies its quest for employees in terms that

Exhibit 5-1. Company missions.

Organization	What it's called	Statement
Bristol-Meyers Squibb Company		Bristol-Myers Squibb is a pharmaceutical and related healthcare products company where the mission is to extend and enhance human life.
Colgate-Palmolive	Three core corporate values	Caring, Global Teamwork, and Continuous Improvement
Fannie Mae	Our public mission	Our public mission, and our defining goal, is to help more families achieve the American Dream of homeownership.
Herman Miller	Background	Herman Miller creates great places to work by researching, designing, manufacturing, and distributing innovative interior furnishings that support companies, organizations, and individuals all over the world.
Minnesota Mining and Manufacturing		We promise innovative and reliable products and services from a company you can trust.
Southwest Airlines	Our Mission Statement	The mission of Southwest Airlines is dedication to the highest quality of Customer Service delivered with a sense of warmth, friendliness, individual pride, and Company Spirit.
Wal-Mart Stores, Inc.	3 Basic Beliefs	1. Respect for the Individual 2. Service to Our Customers 3. Strive for Excellence

encompass both its products and its customers: "If many of us now work more than we climb, and care more for our families than for bumming about, we still sound our appeal to the dirtbag within, the need for the wild dirtbag spirit to survive in our e'd-out culture."

Talent value propositions may respond to the implicit question: How will you persuade me to come work for you? Indeed, some companies incorporate this question in their recruitment advertisements. For example, McKinsey & Company basically tells employees "that they will have to work very hard and that what they will get back is experience working with the cutting edge of the U.S. economy." Amgen has a motto in their employee value proposition that says, "We cheat death"—because employees create drugs that keep people alive who would otherwise be dead. Talent value propositions from these and other companies ranked in *Fortune*'s list of the 100 Best Companies to Work For are presented in Exhibit 5-2.

Distinctive and compelling value propositions can come from organizations in varying industry settings and, as evidenced by Patagonia, with varying employee population sizes. For East Alabama Medical Center (EAMC), a not-for-profit medical system based in rural Opelika, Alabama, a key part of its value proposition is an employee gainsharing compensation program both distinctive to the region's employment community and probably unique among nonprofits nationwide. The program, described in more detail in Chapter 7, enables EAMC and its hiring managers to step above and aside from other employers who generally compete for talent using small differentials in starting base pay.

Talent value propositions don't necessarily have to be sugarcoated. For example, the value proposition for Akibia, a Westborough, Massachusetts–based provider of customer relationship management (CRM) consulting and IT support services is blunt: "No Jerks." The proposition states a value that happens to resonate with Akibia's constituencies of technology talent, talent prospects, and customers in a small, team-based, and customer-focused business. During 2001, the proposition was the guiding motto for Akibia's hiring of 150 people out

Exhibit 5-2. Customer and talent value propositions.

Organization	Customer value proposition	Talent value proposition
1. Amgen	"Use science and innovation to dramatically improve people's lives."	"With the products we create, we make a difference in the lives of patients around the world"
2. American Skandia Life Insurance Corporation	"The company was founded upon the basic principle that innovative and optimistic solutions were better than the status quo that existed in the industry."	"Believers in 'human capital'—that unique capacity to transfer knowledge from one person to another and build a base of talent that generates new ideas and adds value to each and every client relationship."
3. Cisco	Using the Internet to "change the way we work, live, play, and learn."	"Working together to truly shape the way people work, live, play, and learn on the Internet."
4. Charles Schwab & Co., Inc.	"Provide customers with the most useful and ethical financial services in the world."	"By putting new technologies in the hands of talented employees, we help our investors become more educated."

(continues)

Exhibit 5-2. (Continued).

Organization	Customer value proposition	Talent value proposition
5. Container Store	The best selection anywhere plus the best service anywhere plus the best or equal to the best price in our market area.	One great person equals three good people.
6. Patagonia, Inc.	"Environmentally conscious makers of quality outdoor clothing"	"If many of us now work more than we climb, and care more for our families than for bumming about, we still sound our appeal to the dirtbag within, the need for the wild dirtbag spirit to survive in our e'd-out culture."
7. SAS Institute Inc.	"Deliver superior software and services that give people the power to make the right decisions. We want to be the most valued competitive weapon in business decision making."	• "Satisfied employees create satisfied customers • Treating employees like the assets they are • Offering opportunities around the globe • Encouraging employees to be a part of their communities • Supporting a balance between home and work"
8. Southwest Airlines	"We are in the Customer Service business—we just happen to provide airline transportation"	"Feel Free to Actually Enjoy What You Do"

of 2,500 screened. Although prospects were evaluated on many skills and attributes, a "jerk" rating by one Akibia staffer doomed any prospect's chances.

Although a talent value proposition is likely to originate in recruiting and hiring, its impact doesn't stop at the point of hire—it should be only the beginning. The total employment experience—from initial contact, through hiring, employment, and even departure—has a huge influence on the effectiveness of the value proposition. For example, Bain & Co., like McKinsey an international consulting firm headquartered in Boston, maintains alumni relationships with nineteen hundred of its former employees in North America alone, providing them with updated alumni directories, invitations to attend cocktail receptions or to participate in panel discussions, and a biannual newsletter updating them on firm developments and the achievements of other alumni. The talent value proposition to prospective and current employees as well as alumni? We make you marketable.[3]

Employment branding

The concept of brand marketing strategy has been around since 1931 when the heirs of Harley Procter at Procter & Gamble first introduced a brand-focused management system to differentiate its products to customers. Under the system, customer segments were identified, their size estimated, and needs profiles established. Value propositions, pricing strategies, advertising, sales channel, and selling tactics followed.

Something like brand positioning has increasingly been adopted and adapted as a talent strategy, both to create favorable buzz about the employer and to communicate culture and business strategy to potential job applicants. A recent Conference Board study sponsored by Charles Schwab highlights the trend: 40 percent of participating companies reported their intent and efforts to create so-called employer brands, images of their company as a place to work, including the organization's mission, culture, employees, perks, and more.

There are traps to avoid in employer brand positioning. One is the misconception that the employer has complete control over its identity. To one degree or another, the community of applicants, employees, former employees, and others has always had its own—sometimes vague, sometimes explicit; sometime accurate, sometimes inaccurate; sometimes flattering, sometimes unflattering—brand image of the employer. But now the Internet provides explicit branding outlets, where employers can communicate their brands, but where competing insider information is also available.

For example, Vault.com (www.vault.com) allows sponsoring companies to communicate their talent value propositions in the form of Why Work for Us? sections. But Vault also sells information, based on interviews with company employees, about what it is like to work in a particular company. And Vault visitors can link to message boards where current employees post their own opinions of the workplace.

The bottom line is that an employer is no longer a one-way mirror in portraying its value to talent prospects: There is a difference between brand positioning (what you're trying to say about the company) and brand image (how others perceive the company). So a good first step is to determine what these sources have to say about your brand. This is essentially a researching process, gathering information from long-term employees, recent hires, and even prospects that rejected your company's offer. Recent hires in particular can share perceptions of the company before they joined, and whether the reality was consistent with expectations. Why did they choose your workplace over another? How would they suggest marketing your company to other prospects? How would they compare your recruiting process to that of other employers? The goal is not to deny or undo reality by defining brand identity as something it is not; instead, it is important to identify gaps.

Employer of choice

But what can you do about the gaps? One strategy approach that gained popularity at the height of the talent wars is working to become an employer of choice. The phenomenon sometimes goes by other names, like best employers, preferred employers, and great places to work.[4] Nor are there agreed-upon standards for an employer of choice to meet—no single surefire route. Brand positioning remains the underlying objective: Position your workplace in the talent market, as products and services are positioned in their markets. Know your customers. Convince them you are different. Build brand loyalty.

The basic process involves the following three stages:

1. Identifying traits of model employees
2. Figuring out what these people want in a job
3. Seeing to it that these people think they will find it more reliably at your company than anywhere else

Employer-of-choice initiatives can escalate to the art, reach, and logistics of a large advertising campaign—conducting focus groups, polling current employees on what they really want, and conducting competitive benchmarking surveys on pay-and-benefits structures. Short of this, however, real value can be obtained by establishing, through basic grassroots efforts, an accurate, customized measure of what matters most to the talent that matters most.

Such homegrown measures are preferable, we think. Although there is a warehouse of industry research on these issues, the results tend to hover between telling a lot and not telling much at all. Exhibit 5-3 shows the results of a small sample of recent surveys (the oldest in 1993, the most recent in 2001) of varying size, rigor, and issue orientation concerning what is most important to people about work. The results depend, of course, on the questions asked. Some issues seem to come up consistently, through different audiences and contexts: pay, work/family balance, and career growth opportunities. In Exhibit 5-3, survey # 7 is of interest because, in apparent contrast to the other studies, it asks what matters most to high performers—as identified by companies participating in the survey.

The answers depend as well on who is answering and who is asking. As Exhibit 5-4 demonstrates, there may well be a mismatch between what workers value about the workplace and what employers (in this

Exhibit 5-3: What's important to talent?

	1. Why workers leave[1]	2. Drivers of employee retention[2]	3. Ways employees define their ideal job[3]	4. What is most important at work[4]	5. Five issues most important to employees today[5]	6. Reason considered "very important" in taking current job[6]	7. What top-performing employees want[7]
a. Access to decision makers						X	
b. Adequate staffing levels							
c. Autonomy (having power to make decisions affecting your own work)			X	X		X	
d. Balancing work and personal life			X	X	X	X	
e. Being trusted to get the job done			X				
f. Benefit system/benefit level		X				X	
g. Challenging work				X	X	X	
h. Company loyalty to employees	X						

	1	2	3	4	5	6	7
i. Earnings potential with the company	X					X	
j. Fairness/timeliness of salary increases	X		X		X		
k. Job security	X					X	
l. Manager/supervisor behavior/treatment	X		X	X		X	
m. Open communications	X		X			X	
n. Opportunity for career growth and development	X	X	X	X		X	X
o. Passion for employer's mission				X	X		
p. Pay system/pay level	X		X	X	X		X
q. Receiving training that increases skills and abilities		X					
r. Time off	X		X			X	X
s. Type of people/culture							X

1. 1999–2000 Saratoga Institute nationwide study of 9,000 participants in 18 companies, employing between 250 and 8,000 workers: the top five answers to why workers leave.
2. Rewards of Work 2000: What Do Employees Value at Work, a survey of the American workforce, conducted by Sibson Consulting in partnership with WorldatWork; random sample of the U.S. workforce, using telephone survey responses from 1,218 adults; five types of rewards examined in the study are financial rewards; indirect financial rewards (benefits); satisfying work content; affiliation with an admirable organization; and long-term career opportunities.
3. 2001 Randstad North American Employee Review of Job Satisfaction.
4. February 2000 survey of 500 employees asking what was most important to them at work; reported by The Omnia Group, Inc.
5. Selected results from The Discovery Group Normative Database™, a compilation of results from Employee Opinion Surveys conducted for more than 50 organizations representing the views of over 50,000 employees.
6. 1993 Family and Work Institute study of 3,400 employees.
7. Fifth annual (2000) Watson Wyatt Strategic Rewards® survey. Employers participating in the survey were asked to identify their top performers and invite them to measure and rank their opinions about the effectiveness of various reward programs.

Exhibit 5-4. What's important to talent (II)? Top five qualities employees cite as most important in their work vs. top five factors as perceived by HR professionals.

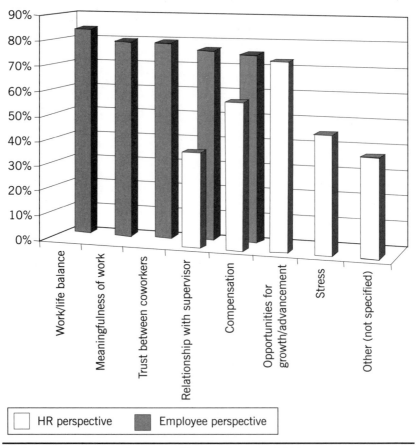

Based on data from a survey by Development Dimensions International (DDI)

case HR professionals) perceive they value. In this particular instance, talent and HR perceptions overlapped on only two factors—relationship with supervisor and compensation.

Even assumptions about generational preferences can fall apart. For example, a study conducted in late 2000 and focusing specifically on generation X talent—thirteen hundred men and women born between 1964 and 1975 and employed at eight U.S. and two Canadian companies—found these assumption-defying results: 70 percent of the surveyed workers rated companionship, a loving family, and enjoying life as extremely important, while fewer than 20 percent said earning a lot of money and becoming an influential leader were extremely important goals.[5] And, conditioned on that sort of workplace environment, 47 percent of the respondents reported they would be happy to spend the rest of their careers at their current organizations.

Employer-of-choice processes often result in sculpting or fine-tuning what might be called relational or environmental employment factors. Sometimes this involves offsetting chronic but unavoidable employment irritations with visibly compensating benefits. For example, a business that looks at its workforce and sees time-pressed men and women from dual-earner families may offer benefits that communicate family friendliness.

This approach is particularly apt for professional services companies in areas such as law, management consulting, and IT consulting, where demand for long hours, extensive travel, and drop-everything availability is notorious but also often the norm. Palo Alto–based law firm Fenwick & West LLP, for example, is particularly explicit in communicating work programs and options to offset some of these demands. The firm publishes on its Web career pages (www.fenwick.com) the base salary levels for Bay Area associates in years one through seven opting to work at a minimum annual level of 1,950 billable hours. The firm also provides an alternative compensation schedule for attorneys opting to work between 1,800 and 1,950 hours annually. The law firm permits up to fifty annual hours of pro bono work to be counted toward billable hour totals. And, finally, for staff attorneys, paralegals, and legal secretaries, the firm provides weekend-getaway retreat programs.

Employer-of-choice and other brand positioning efforts risk a second trap: the illusion that an employer brand—whether good, bad, or indifferent—has meaningful reach and consequence. This is often a matter of scale. The reality is that most employers cannot and should not aspire to creating a national or even a regional brand. According to one economic researcher's estimate, only about 40 percent of U.S. employees are in companies large and established enough to have a visible reputation in their communities.[6]

But this reality doesn't argue against talent value propositions. It simply says that branding expectation should be kept realistic and within the bounds of business strategies. It also says that the value propositions should be tailored—explicitly segmented—to fit critical talent niches.

Strategy objectives and initiatives

Talent strategies, like business strategies, require destinations—strategy objectives. Talent strategy objectives describe the end results of planned activities, quantified if possible. Setting them down requires grasping the implications of business strategy objectives for people—and transforming those implications into strategy-supporting objectives and initiatives. Among the contexts in which talent strategy objectives might be set, are:

- Progress toward attainment of key organization competencies
- Reduction of defections among highly valued talent
- Improved customer service evaluations based on interactions with frontline talent
- Reduced time-to-market for products and services based on talent factors such as competencies, reduced turnover, and reward-based incentives
- Increased proportion of employee referral-based hires among total hires
- Enhanced revenue and product revenue mix traced to changes in sales incentive reward programs
- Reduced temp and contractor costs attributed to work process engineering or cross-training initiatives
- Improved communication of strategy objectives via performance management initiatives (for example, as measured via a survey of strategy knowledge)

Setting objectives and choosing strategy initiatives involves trade-offs. In any business setting ideas pour in every day; however, some ideas will be inconsistent with business strategies, structure, or culture, still others will require unavailable resources or unacceptable timelines. It is important to enforce trade-offs by filtering input through the prism of strategy objectives, and to keep objectives to a significant, manageable few.

Although it is also important that setting strategy objectives precede consideration of alternative strategy initiatives, in practice that often does not happen. After all, the bias of business is to be decisive—to avoid paralysis by analysis and act. But bypassing objective setting ends up being a way of letting program and resource choices set objectives—instead of having planned activities incorporate clear objectives.[7]

There are a number of ways to ensure that objective setting is intentional, while not becoming bogged down in inactivity. One way is to use prestrategy assessment information (see Exhibit 4-8) to create a strategy objectives matrix similar to Exhibit 5-5. The matrix balances internal talent strengths and weaknesses against external market threats and opportunities. In addition to making objective setting deliberate, using the matrix has two further advantages. First, it enables follow-through on the information that hopefully was collected through internal and external scanning. (If that information does not point to important, clear objectives—or points to too many—it is a sign that more or better information needs to be obtained.) Second, because the matrix displays strengths, weaknesses, opportunities, and threats on one sheet of paper, it is possible to prioritize objectives, such as:

- Setting objectives that use internal strengths to capitalize on external opportunities
- Setting objectives that use external opportunities to improve internal weaknesses
- Setting objectives that pit internal strengths against external threats
- Avoiding objectives that attempt to match external threats with internal weaknesses

Exhibit 5-5. Setting strategy objectives.

	Strengths (S)	Weaknesses (W)
	• Strong retention rates during first year of employment	• New sales staff lacks significant industry experience
	• Solid results from staff survey of product knowledge, strategy understanding	• Pay benchmarks lagging
Opportunities (O)	**SO Strategy Objectives**	**WO Strategy Objectives**
• Favorable press about recent product release successes	•	•
• Recent downsizing by competitor XYZ	•	•
Threats (T)	**ST Strategy Objectives**	**WT Strategy Objectives**
• New product releases giving technology and product management staff visibility	•	•
• Key technology leaders being contacted by search companies	•	•

Mapping strategy objectives and initiatives

A second objective-setting technique is to map business objectives that incorporate strategy objectives and initiatives. Why use maps? The reason is simple: Clear information is an essential and timeless strategy ingredient, and maps are the essence of information. At the U.S. Military Academy at West Point, for example, map reading is the only course still being taught today that was taught when West Point was first founded in 1802.

For our purposes, mapping strategy objectives is simply a way of diagramming and understanding a causal chain of events—how business plans lead to business results, how talent strategy objectives and initiatives contribute to and interact with business plans. Used in this context, even simple maps can be compelling tools for strategy visualizing, objective setting, describing, revising, communicating, and consensus building.

Maps in a typical American business are usually constrained to maps of tangible—financial and physical—assets, such as:

- An organization chart—a map of divisions, functions, departments, and leaders
- An income statement, and
- A balance sheet—both maps of its financial resources

These maps are fundamental. But they also have their limitations, especially in that they are static and retrospective. In the arena of business strategy, mapping is making inroads as an accepted planning and measurement tool, for example, in balanced scorecard initiatives.[8] (See Chapter 8 for a discussion of so-called balanced measures.)

Talent strategies involve the creation and deployment of intangibles—for instance, recruiting relationships, talent competencies, learning and knowledge, customer relationships, performance levels, commitment and motivation. While the deployment value of physical and financial resources can be captured in spreadsheets and budget reports, capturing the deployment value of human capital is more difficult. Less important than the separate value of each intangible asset are the value of the entire set and the strategy that links and orchestrates them. In this sense, talent strategy maps can describe how assumptions, resources, and tactics are believed to interact to produce strategy deliverables.

A basic strategy map is displayed in Exhibit 5-6. The clear boxes in the exhibit depict causal business strategy relationships that link:

- Enhanced customer management processes to →
- Operational excellence to →
- Increased customer value to →
- Revenue growth to →
- Increased shareholder value

The shaded boxes add two talent strategy relationships that link:

- Customer relationship learning initiatives to →
- Customer relationship competencies →

And then to enhanced customer management processes.

This is a simple example, but maps can be drawn to include many more factors and interactions. Whatever the level of detail, it is important that mapped relationships not be assumed. In extending business strategy impact to talent factors, strategy builders should dig deep to understand precisely how talent creates value and exactly how valuable is its contribution. The question is, "What causes what in the relationship?" Not just that more learning is good, but how does learning affect revenues: What is the specific evidence? What are the steps along the way?

It is also important to note, in anticipation of Chapters 6, 7, and 8, that strategy maps can be used beyond talent strategy building into the strategy delivery and measurement stages. One of the fundamental challenges of an economy that is both customer-driven and talent-intensive is providing employees with better, clearer information on what they should be doing and why it is important. Organization charts do not tell

Exhibit 5-6. Strategy map example.

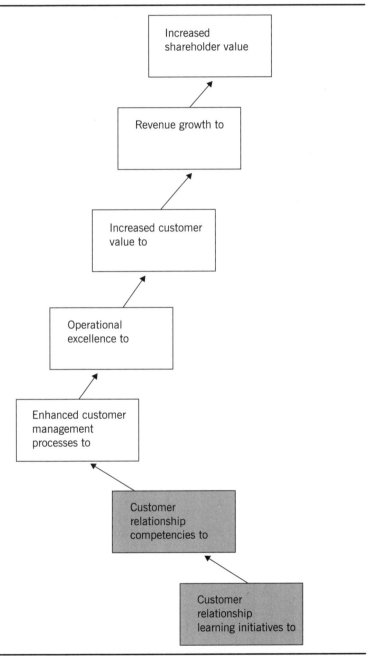

Increased
shareholder value

Revenue growth to

Increased customer
value to

Operational
excellence to

Enhanced customer
management
processes to

Customer
relationship
competencies to

Customer
relationship
learning initiatives to

this story; financial statements perhaps do, but for a limited audience. Clear written explanations may be effective, though it is particularly challenging to communicate a business strategies narrative that is both concise and compelling. Here strategy maps can be powerful tools to illustrate, in visual terms, how talent strategy value propositions, strategy objectives, processes, and initiatives come together (for example, in Exhibit 5-6, the ultimate connection between customer relationship learning and increased shareholder value).

Measurable objectives

Objectives are destinations—it is important to quantify the destination, know how far you've got to go, and when you arrive. Objectives without measures are useless. It is important to design measurement processes that convincingly showcase the impact of talent investments on business performance. We defer most of our discussion about measures of strategies and programs to Chapter 8. But being attuned here to measurement, or more precisely, to measurability, is an important aspect of the objective-setting process.

Aligning talent strategy objectives

Talent strategy objectives and initiatives cannot be devised or delivered in a vacuum: They require internal consistency—what we'll call *horizontal alignment*. Equally important, if not more so, they require external consistency with business strategies—or vertical alignment. Finally, they require market alignment with the realities of both the current and anticipated market for talent.

Horizontal alignment.   Internal or horizontal alignment means that talent functions, processes, and objectives are on the same page. Talent flow processes, talent engagement processes, and their supporting systems reinforce one another and send consistent—or at least not contradictory—messages. Enabling links exist among efforts to source, screen, select, develop, and deploy and the performance competencies required to implement business strategy objectives. Rewards, performance management, and employee support services are in place to alert, to attract high performance talent to the business, to motivate and commit them while employed, and to continue them as a contingent resource beyond traditional employment.

Examples of misalignment are often not difficult to spot—at least when put in the context of what has to happen to make the talent aspects of business strategy work. The difficulty is more often in countering the momentum of established practices and ways of thinking. For example, the business may need to acquire talent for long-term development and high-performance levels, yet recruiting processes and resources are invariably geared to the lowest cost per hire. Or the company may expect employees to work together collaboratively in teams while performance management and reward processes exclusively encourage individual performance contributions. Often, rather than being intentional, misalignments such as these may result from policies and practices developed over time and independently of one another. And here it is not just a matter of the policies and practices on paper—the misalignment may result from how they are interpreted and administered. This lack of intention, however, does not make their practical and administrative roots any less deep. Indeed, removing the obstacles to better internal alignment may be necessary initial talent strategy objectives.

Vertical alignment.   Talent strategies that are inconsistent with business strategies are costly. According to a 2002 benchmark study of HR best practices from Hackett Best Practices, HR organizations squander an average of 56 percent of their budget when they focus on initiatives that are not aligned with company business priorities.

Yet achieving and sustaining alignment is not easy; and it becomes particularly difficult if there are conflicts in communication, trust, and other partnering factors among business leaders and HR leaders. Achieving alignment often has less to do with strategy content or prioritizing, and more to do with interpersonal and collaboration factors such as:

- Strong leadership and support from senior management
- Mutual understanding of both business and talent environments
- Delivering on commitments
- Good cross-functional or cross-process working relationships based on trust and effective communications
- Effective joint prioritization of effort and resources
- Demonstration of leadership and influencing (horizontal leadership) qualities

Moving forward will be evolutionary, requiring sustainable beliefs, behaviors, dialogue, and feedback that support the gap-closing process. Indeed, efforts to improve factors such as strategy alignment are also legitimate talent strategies objectives.

Talent market alignment.   One of the frustrating but unavoidable ironies is that when business strategies are poised to deliver tremendous success, the going tends to be roughest for talent strategies. Business strategies flourish when business conditions are best. But at these times, employment markets tend to become sellers' markets and talent strategy objectives run into costlier, more difficult recruiting and costlier, more damaging turnover.

Because market alignment is a moving target, a certain amount of counter cyclical, or "what if," thinking needs to go into the building of strategy objectives, especially when objectives involve long-term commitments and resource bets. For example, in a 1998 article published as the hiring demand for IT professionals seemed to be heading through the roof, we suggested that: "Strategy works best when the future is seen as being right in front of you and the present is looked at from a distance."[9] At the time, looking close up at the future involved such contrarian recommendations as:

- Consider exit strategies as well as entry strategies when it comes to creative compensation.

- Research, understand, and plan for the impact of alternative IT staffing arrangements such as outsourcing.

However, talent strategy objectives should not ignore the realities of current resources, business conditions, and talent market conditions—for example, by investing heavily in recruiting infrastructure in the midst of intensive reductions or abandoning retention initiatives just as the talent marketplace heats up. Objectives should be tested, at least informally, and under at least a couple of alternative scenarios; which will have some bearing on the confidence level attached to the objectives. And, should a realistic alternative future threaten to invalidate important talent strategy objectives and initiatives, this will give you a chance to consider a transition plan.

Market alignment also involves being alert to inflection points, that is, places where established trends in employment demand or other market trends shift. Some of these changes can be seen in regional or national economy: For example, a marked shift, up or (as in January 2002) down, in the number of initial claims for unemployment benefits, considered a strong leading indicator both for the economy and the talent marketplace. Other changes are homegrown: Employment offers that were routinely accepted now get routinely turned down, or there are sudden and unanticipated defections of crucial talent.

Finally, let us say that market alignment should not be viewed as the final arbiter and not every market blip is an inflection point. We are talking strategies here. Sometimes it may be necessary to go "against the herd" to sustain strategic processes against the latest, seemingly strong pull of the market. A business downturn might prompt a change in talent process focus—in talent flow, for example, from sourcing to screening—but it shouldn't force the shutdown of strategic processes.

Strategy athletes

We began this chapter by arguing that merely having a talent mindset was not enough to propel purposeful and successful talent strategies in a company. We return to the notion here to describe two versions of talent mind-set. Both versions are important. One is more heralded but is beyond the scope of this book. The second, we found, is among the primary reasons that talent-based strategies succeed.

The first version of talent mind-set clearly comes from the top. For example, business executive leaders such as Herb Kelleher at Southwest Airlines, Jim Goodnight of SAS, and Jack Welch former CEO of GE (who transformed himself from being an analytically driven planning strategist to a talent strategy champion) have become personal exemplars of their companies' talent strategies. In such cases, it is impossible to replicate the essence of the leader's strategy driving personality. It is also difficult to benchmark and transplant wholesale the talent strategies and practices that resulted from the leader's influence. Intertwined, the person and the policies combine subtly and inextricably to make the strategies and the talent value propositions.

The second type of talent mind-set, to be explored in the next pages, is something a bit different. Business strategies and talent strategies are ultimately conceived, built, implemented, and sustained by talent athletes. These leader-managers possess a talent mind-set; they are also adept in envisioning, creating, leading, and continually fine-tuning action plans and resources devoted to talent strategy initiatives.

Notes

1. Ed Michaels, Helen Handfield-Jones, and Beth Axelrod, *The War for Talent* (Boston: Harvard Business School Press, 2001), p. x.

2. Robert S. Kaplan and David P. Norton, "Having Trouble with Your Strategy? Then Map It," *Harvard Business Review*, September–October 2000, p. 171.

3. Scott Kirsner, "Hire Today, Gone Tomorrow?" *Fast Company*, August 1998, p. 136.

4. These concepts have surfaced visibly as best employer lists in a number of specialty business publications and for career-oriented trade/professional organizations. While criteria vary for employers aspiring to a place on one or more

of these lists, employers must usually nominate themselves; complete a lengthy questionnaire; and submit key measurement data on employment factors such as pay, benefits, training, promotional opportunities, turnover, and workforce diversity. Some lists include a test of employer claims via surveys completed by employees. An external evaluative firm, sometimes with the collaboration of employers who have already made the list, usually coordinates the process. Final rankings are often determined by computer analysis/calculation of a series of weighted factors.

For employers, including small employers, hoping to establish their employment brand among particular constituencies, these lists continue to be effective branding tools. Some examples of these best-places-to-work lists include:

- *Fortune*'s list of the 100 Best Companies to Work For
- *Fortune*'s The 50 Best Companies for Minorities
- *Computerworld*'s 100 Best Places to Work in IT
- *Latina Style* magazine's 50 Best Companies for Latinas to Work for in the U.S.
- National Association for Female Executives' (NAFE) Top 25 Companies for Executive Women
- *Women's Wire*'s Best Companies for Women
- *Working Mother*'s The 100 Best Companies for Working Mothers

5. Maggie Jackson, "For Many Generation X'ers, Job Loyalty Is Getting Stronger," *The New York Times,* December 11, 2001, p. C2.

6. However, being a large company is not always a prerequisite. For example, companies such as The Container Store and Patagonia are relatively small in terms of employee population. But the fact that they have retailing brand names, and have been featured on the *Fortune* list of Best Companies to Work For, helps to establish an employer brand as well.

7. B.B. Tregoe and J.W. Zimmermann, "The New Strategic Manager," *Business,* May–June 1981, p. 19.

8. Kaplan and Norton, pp. 168–169.

9. David Sears, "Staffing the New Economy: Shortage or Myth?" *HR Magazine,* June 1998, p. 136.

CHAPTER 6

◪ TALENT FLOW STRATEGIES

S TRATEGIES ARE NEARLY ALWAYS WORKS in progress, and it is no less so with strategy delivery than it is with strategy planning. Describing talent strategies or strategy initiatives at a point in time usually reveals unevenness—some components ahead or behind others, or a concentration of effort in one area at the apparent expense of others. And that was what we found as we talked to business leaders—many of them, but not all, in HR—and heard them describe their business environments, their talent market circumstances, their visions, their talent-based strategy initiatives, and progress.

Signature talent strategy successes

We didn't encounter completed sets of strategies, or ones that weren't making trade-offs, or ones that completely balanced the interests of talent flow and talent engagement. This seems hardly surprising when we consider an estimate from the Balanced Scorecard Collaborative that 80 percent of HR organizations lack a strategic plan of any sort for connecting talent resource allocations to enterprise strategies. And this statistic isn't surprising when we think about the eternal scarcity of resources; the need to take first things first; and the importance of identifying, honing, and leveraging one or a few distinctive competencies. (As strategy thought leader Michael Porter describes it: "You don't have to have all the answers up front. Most successful companies get two or three or four of the pieces right at the start, and then they elucidate their strategy over time."[1])

What we often end up focusing on are signature talent strategy successes. These initiatives stand out because they are in natural synch with the strategic direction of the business—for example, talent value propositions that fit glovelike with customer value propositions, as is the case for Patagonia or the Container Store or Akibia—or because they are successful in mastering organization constraints that often prevent the best ideas from happening, or because they leverage the realities faced by companies in their talent market, or because they point the way to other strategic initiatives. For example, as director of recruiting and development, Tom Gloudeman's facilitation/communication role during the building of Lands' End's five-year strategic plan leverages his value in both recruiting and professional development processes as the plan rolls out. This in turn enabled making a business case for talent competency building, a talent strategy work in progress described later in this chapter. For Rebecca Ray, senior vice president and director of training for American Skandia, envisioning, building, and successfully rolling out a corporate university initiative on a tight schedule, and with limited external resources, has opened doors to extend American Skandia's financial services learning capabilities beyond traditional enterprise boundaries.

Delivering flawless transactions

We also focused on organizations that get the talent basics right—or at least are well along the path of getting them right. Often the biggest constraint that talent strategy initiatives must overcome is a history or a reputation—or, at worst, an ongoing reality—of administrative ineptitude.

HR leaders increasingly need to operate at both administrative and strategic levels. Transactional work is still the bane of HR's existence. Although there is a growing trend toward isolating and outsourcing nonstrategic HR administration, and while we believe talent-based strategies are make-or-break strategic issues in most businesses, efforts to bypass or off-load transactions in favor of strategy initiatives have never proved to be the way to the strategy table.[2] In fact, mastering transactions is usually the price of admission. One HR leader we talked to likened talent-based strategies to "the mountain" and transactions to "base camp." "It's great to leave camp for the ascent, but it's a stage you have to reach before the climb . . . and you can't leave it until you're ready."

Persistent flaws in the delivery of transaction-based work damage the credibility and legitimacy HR leaders and professionals need in order to advance strategic agendas. A University of Michigan study confirms that this personal credibility is a key factor in how businesspeople assess HR competency: More than 60 percent of personal credibility is a function of doing what was promised and delivering error-free work.

This reality certainly reflects the strategy delivery approaches of the leaders we interviewed. One representative example is the way the HR vice president for a *Fortune* 1000 publishing and information services company layers the delivery of his group's operations and strategies under the company's three-year plan:

- A foundation layer of maintaining, improving, or perfecting transaction delivery

- A second layer of cross-organizational talent strategy process initiatives; in his case, the implementation of an enhanced performance communication and management program
- A layer of proactive initiatives in support of emerging business strategy issues; in his case, the talent implications of new publishing technologies and new product categories

Communicating strategies

When we asked the HR vice president for a broadband telecommunications company how his business strategy was communicated to employees, he admitted quickly and with frustration that it was not communicated very well. The executive went on to describe elaborate, costly, and ultimately unsuccessful efforts to put the strategy into words to communicate to the company's employees. The management team never reached agreement on terminology, timing, or communication channels. Efforts to do so went around in circles. As a result, business strategy was never fully or consistently communicated.

This is not a rare case. In fact, it may be a common theme in the postmortems of many failed business strategies. It may well have played a role in this particular company's demise. Although having both technology and infrastructure that were state-of-the-art and a solid customer base, the company had trouble serving its customers, and struggled with inadequate billing and customer service systems. Its value in bankruptcy plunged from a multibillion plateau down to tens of millions. And all but a few hundred of its workers were laid off.

Human resources has or should have a direct role in formulating and delivering business strategy communicating, not only in words but also in policies, processes, incentive decisions, and actions. To the extent that a business' workforce needs to understand business strategy—and to the extent that this understanding has a bearing on the many thousands of things that get done in an organization every day—these are strategic responsibilities.

Strategy communication, and employee communication in general, seem to come easier in smaller start-up companies. For example, in a survey of 570 HR professionals conducted jointly by the Society for Human Resources Management and Fisher College of Business at Ohio State University, 73 percent of those in start-ups report that superiors keep open communication with employees. By contrast, only 50 percent of those in more established companies said the same.[3]

The reasons that strategies are not communicated are legion. A few examples—and their counterpoints—are listed in Exhibit 6-1. Many companies think they communicate strategy under phrases such as "world-class customer service" or "stakeholder satisfaction" or "total quality." Such strategy sloganeering, if it is the sum total of communication, leaves people without assembly and operating instructions—the details and motivation to take action. It is often confusing activities with strategies. Strategies are what a business does to distinguish itself, to

Exhibit 6-1. Reasons why strategies don't get communicated.

Point:	Counterpoint:
• Actual and potential competitors might learn about "shop secrets"	Business strategies aren't the same as trade secrets, secret formulas, budget plans, even operational results.
• It's too complicated	This implies that people in the business can't understand the goals that their efforts in some way should achieve. Strategy doesn't have to equal complexity. It's important to clarify and hone strategy, not obscure it.
• Business conditions and the strategies change so often	Strategies are about the customers a business serves and the basic value it delivers to those customers. If this lacks continuity, not only is it hard for the people in your organization to grasp what the strategies are, it's hard as well for customers to know and believe what your business stands for.

gain and sustain a competitive advantage. Strategies are not slogans such as "world-class customer service" or "defect-free manufacturing" that companies must do just to keep the doors open.

One classic example of rigorous, multichannel strategy communication processes are those initiated under Emerson Electric's chairperson and former CEO, Charles F. Knight. The processes include a clear definition of business achievement expressed in unambiguous financial measures; a common vocabulary, with critical operational terms (*best cost producer*, for example); and decision rules intended to inform behavior from executive offices to the factory floors. Every manager and worker at Emerson is expected to be able to answer four basic questions about his or her work: Who is the competitor? Do you understand the economics of your job? What cost reduction are you currently working on? Have you met with your managers in the past six months?

A second, still-evolving example is the communication practices of the Container Store, the Dallas-based retailer ranked second in *Fortune* magazine's 2001 best companies list. The Container Store's strategies are embodied in six foundation principles that blend business strategies, talent strategies, and customer service practices. The principles are included in the employee handbook, but also provide the foundation for the Container Store's talent value proposition and its substantial training programs for both in-store and logistics talent.

A third ingenious strategy communication example employs a variation of the mapping process introduced in Chapter 5. In 1998, when restaurant franchiser Taco Bell devised a customer service-focused turn-around strategy to distinguish itself from other big chains, its management team realized that strategy execution would hinge on the ability and willingness of Taco Bell's frontline leaders—its seven thousand restaurant managers—to understand the strategy and accept responsibility for translating the strategy into day-to-day reality. To launch its strategy implementation process, Taco Bell convened 90 percent of the managers in Nashville. The group was split into teams of about ten managers each, and each team was given a map called "Welcome to the Jungle," a colorful information graphic using metaphor, imagery, and data to capture strategic dilemmas. The map identified pitfalls faced by the company and its managers in delivering the Taco Bell Promise: "To be the most energizing place to work, eat, and own."

With franchise owners, vice presidents, directors, and district managers acting as coaches, the restaurant managers then navigated a series of mapping exercises, each of which asked participants to draw conclusions from information that was presented to them. Using the process, many managers for the first time understood where the company stood in relation to its competition, what percentage of restaurant managers were making their goals, and what their stores needed to work on.[4]

Talent flow

Talent flow processes consist of recruiting, retention, and pre- and post-employment relationships. Of the three, recruiting has perhaps undergone the most noticeable transformation, due to the unprecedented impact of information technology. During the past few years—driven by the Internet and characterized by so-called information transparency, which benefits both skill buyers and skill sellers—there has been an explosion of tools, processes, resources, and services available to support and accelerate (or, conversely, to bog down and confuse) the recruiting process.

At the other end of the traditional employment relationship, companies deal with the sometimes weak and sometimes overwhelming pull of the talent marketplace. Understanding that there are lost opportunities and costs associated with talent turnover—but not always understanding the magnitude of the costs or the options for reducing them—companies have fashioned retention programs intended to resist that pull.

At both ends of the relationship, business leaders responsible for talent strategies are beginning to see the benefits of relationship building and relationship keeping. Talent relationship strategy initiatives are relatively new to some organizations, while deep-rooted, pragmatic—

although perhaps unacknowledged—processes exist in others. Where they operate or evolve, talent relationship strategies recognize the twin realities that key talent has lives both before and after employment with any one company; and, in the new talent marketplace, what goes around is very apt to come around. Talent relationships seem poised to play an increasingly important role in the talent and employment marketplaces, by smoothing both the acceleration and deceleration of talent flow.

Talent flow resources

By most measures, the business of stocking organizations with talent is a massive undertaking. Consider the following numbers:

- U.S. companies' total 2001 spending on recruitment advertising, while down 35 percent from the previous year, was still a substantial $5.7 billion—about $45 for every working person in the United States. For newspapers, recruitment advertising revenues continues to make the difference between profitability and red ink during most years.
- Domestic U.S. revenue from online advertising and job postings surged 38 percent, to $727 million. The online share of the recruitment advertising market, now at just over 10 percent of the total, is expected to climb to 25 percent within three years.[5]
- By one estimate, the staffing services industry segment inclusive of retained search, contingency search, temp-to-permanent search, and temporary staffing realizes estimated annual revenues exceeding $115 billion, and is growing at an estimated annual percentage rate of about 13 percent. The industry segment employs upwards of four hundred fifty thousand professionals. (See Exhibit 6-2.)
- Annual expenditures for U.S. corporate recruiting, which include the costs of employed HR recruiting staff as well as their contract recruiters, exceed $25 billion.[6] (See Exhibit 6-2.) While this is an estimate dwarfed by expenditures for external recruiting, it has been growing, at least through 2001, at a much steeper rate.

Exhibit 6-2. Estimated revenue/expenditure growth trends in U.S. staffing.

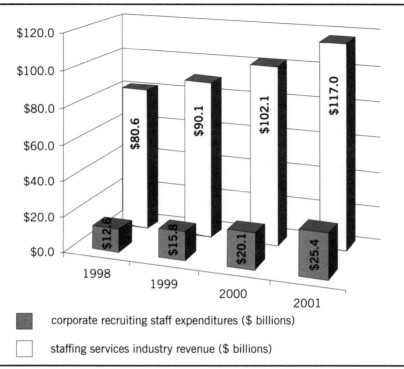

corporate recruiting staff expenditures ($ billions)

staffing services industry revenue ($ billions)

Based on data from *Recruiter Magazine*. Sourcing: Staffing Analysts Inc. estimates based on data from U.S. Bureau of Labor Statistics, Summit Resources, American Staffing Association, National Technical Services Association, National Association of Professional Employer Organizations, National Association of Computer Consultant Businesses, U.S. Census Bureau, SI Review, and Fordyce Letter.

- During 1999 and 2000, U.S. business organizations spent approximately $1 billion acquiring and deploying applicant tracking systems (ATS)—software-based systems to manage the receipt, storage, evaluation, processing, and administration of job information, applicant information, and recruiting transaction information.

Meanwhile, at the micro level, where businesses are most concerned with the efficiencies and productivity of their recruiting processes, the emphasis seems to shift to measuring, tracking, and reporting efficiency through low incremental costs—cost per hire, for example.

The question is: Between these macroestimates and micrometrics, where does the money go?[7] What is often lacking is a perspective on the amounts in the middle: the very substantial budget amounts that are deployed year in and year out—strategically, tactically, or wastefully—for the purpose of communicating employment opportunities, sourcing people to be considered for them, and evaluating and enticing people to take them on.

Data from a survey conducted during 2001 by a partnership between the Society for Human Resources Management (SHRM) and Staffing.org gave a sense of how much organizations spend as well as how they channel resources for talent stocking and replenishment.[8] The data cover organizations of varying sizes in different industries and in different regions of the United States. While the data are a sample and depend for their accuracy on the self-reporting of participating companies, they provide insights into the magnitude, missed opportunities, and strategic impact of recruiting resources. For example:

- The average annual recruiting expenditure for the 679 companies responding was slightly over $6 million, with even small companies (those with less than 100 employees) spending on average nearly $1.3 million, and those with five thousand or more employees spending on average nearly $48 million.
- The sixty-four financial services companies (banking, investment, and mutual fund organizations) participating in the survey reported spending an average of nearly $20 million annually on recruiting costs; insurance organizations (life and auto carriers) reported spending an average of over $12.5 million.
- Average recruiting expenditures by company range roughly between $4 million and $6 million in most U.S. geographic regions, but balloon to an average of nearly $15.5 million in the Southwest (Arizona, California, Colorado, Hawaii, Nevada, New Mexico, Utah, and the territories of Guam and Northern Mariana).
- Looking at it in quantitative terms, survey results suggest that the costs of recruiting at small-size (under 100 employees) to

medium-size (500 to 2,500 employees) companies are disproportionately expensive and underleveraged when compared with
large employers.

- Recruiting expenditures at small- and medium-size companies
  are weighted heavily toward internal efforts (internal or contracted expenses such as salaries, office space, and supplies) and
  produce costs-per-hire that are nearly 100 percent greater than
  those at larger companies.[9]
- For all the hiring challenges and excesses reported from the high-
  tech sector in recent years, data from this survey suggest respect-
  ably low per hire costs ($3,854).
- Comparatively tougher challenges seem to be experienced by the
  healthcare sector. While per organization recruiting costs may be
  modest (around $3 million), the bulk of them (67.4 percent) go to
  external resources, and the resources produce relatively high-cost
  hires ($7,305).
- Where employees are a direct revenue source, for example, in
  consulting, businesses seem to readily accept high recruiting
  costs, high costs-per-hiring, and an apparent trade-off between
  efficiency and time-to-hire. The results for this sector seem to
  show a willing reliance on external recruiting resources (59.5 percent go for outside services as opposed to an average of 43.9 percent across all industries) and a cost-per-hire that averages
  $11,209 (more than twice the industry-wide average of $4,523).

The budgets for talent recruiting resources often end up underesti-
mating an organization's actual investment because of the distributive
nature of the process—especially the obvious and substantial role for
hiring managers in the screening and selection processes. Such resource
budgets, aside from internal infrastructure, often are limited to recruitment advertising and the use of external search services.

While recruiting may seem to be a low-investment proposition, the
truth is that capital and process requirements are significant. Even the
simplest recruiting operations require tools and processes that may not

be initially apparent. Recruiting failure often involves failure to meet underlying budget needs—or too much success in submerging what is actually being spent so that organizations tolerate and waste resources on futilely disjointed recruiting activities, instead of operating integrated strategic talent acquisition processes.

Recruiting

Results from a survey conducted by consulting firm Watson Wyatt indicate that successful recruiting can have the highest impact of any talent management process. A company conducting a strategically focused recruiting program can increase the company's total market value by upwards of 10 percent. High impact here speaks to both efficiency and hiring quality. The people who impact a company's value are high-quality hires who have the potential to produce many times more than the average or low performer.

Despite its potential impact, the substantial company-level resources allocated to it, and the array of new tools and technologies available to support it, very little has changed in the underlying recruiting model used by most employers. During flush times, employers hire vigorously, building up and locking in "just in case" talent inventories.

During the most recent talent wars, tactics and technologies collectively termed *e-cruiting* (online posting, job boards, career portals, research tactics) emerged to support companies with their aggressive hiring plans. The Internet became the most visible and most trafficked venue of the employment marketplace. From 1998 to 2000, for example, the proportion of unemployed workers who reported regularly using the Internet to search for jobs increased from 15 to 26 percent. By 2000, the Internet was populated with more than three thousand job boards; at the height of the talent wars, the total reached thirty thousand, many of them backed by venture capital and, increasingly, by newspapers. Monster.com, still the largest of them all, saw the number of job seeker visits to its site double in less than a year, from 7 million in April 2000 to 14 million in March 2001. In January 2002, according to technology research company Jupiter Media Metrix, 13.9 million people in the

United States still visited Monster.com at least once a month. Job seeking is currently the second most popular activity on the Internet.

E-cruiting technologies and tactics, however, have often been used as process-engineered, high-speed accessories for an old recruiting model. When talent demand seemed to outstrip supply, so-called early adopter companies (many themselves information-technology based) enjoyed temporary tactical advantage using e-cruiting. Ultimately, however, the market and other employers caught up to erase and commoditize the advantage. The end result was the same for both early adopter and late arriver. On the demand side, as the talent marketplace came back to earth, employers had talent warehouses stocked with inventory, some of which had to be liquidated through layoffs. Meanwhile, on the supply side, ease of delivery (34 percent of *Fortune* 500 companies now require that job seekers respond online, up from 27 percent in 2000) enabled the volume of inbound resumes to continue without regard to demand. In fact, e-cruiting now often seems best at overproducing resumes in proportion to the actual number of opportunities.

E-cruiting has transformed the recruitment industry and is moving toward dominance as the primary channel for talent sourcing. All companies that use it as a sourcing medium potentially benefit from its streamlined processes (though many as quickly lose the benefit when electronic submissions run up against more traditional turnarounds of internal screening and selection processes). But, for most companies, e-cruiting by itself no longer qualifies as a distinguishing talent strategy initiative. Among the talent strategy initiatives we consider here, two characteristics stand out:

- The use of competencies to connect talent with essential business competencies in recruiting and other talent processes
- The building and maintaining of pre- and postemployment relationships to create "just in time" talent reserves instead of "just in case" talent inventories

Using talent competencies

Some of the best emerging strategy initiatives to recruit and select people who'll thrive in your company involve a simple but fundamental process: identify the important characteristics of talent who are already thriving and hire others just like them.

In Chapter 4, determining company competencies was described as an essential preliminary step to strategy building. We distinguished between *business-level* competencies and *work-level* competencies. The short list of business-level competencies incorporates distinctive benefits that characterize the company to its customers—that are, in effect, its personality.[10] Business-level competencies provide the context for work-level competencies. Competency models—organized sets of work-level competencies—in turn form the foundation for talent management processes, most often beginning with recruiting.

Competency models define a success-based or results-based view of work. Models are based less on describing what is done on the job and more on the characteristics that lead to successful work performance. The first key requirement is gaining an understanding, in both quantitative and qualitative detail, of the most important work process results. What does success look like? What are the work-level factors that most contribute to success? Competencies affect almost every process in a company. While an enormous amount of time and energy may be devoted to strategy, vision, finance, and marketing, in the end competencies carry the day.

With a working definition of the term *success* and the factors that contribute to it, the next requirement is to determine what separates excellent performers (in specific work assignments, for example, or process roles, or organizational level) from those who do not succeed. This information often comes from interviews, or focus groups: with talent who exemplify success, with managers who witness it, and from strategy-level leaders who know what kind of performance success will be required as the company's strategy unfolds in the future.

These interviews should yield a prioritized list of competencies for recruiting and selecting talent. Sometimes cognitive or intellectual capabilities—gathering information, developing solutions, process expertise, or financial acumen—may top the list. Other times, personality attributes—relating to people, influencing outcomes, persistence, or adapting to change—may be more important. To ensure the validity of competencies—that they indeed correlate with superior job performance—both successful employees and less successful employees may be evaluated further. For example, cognitive tests may be administered to verify that successful talent in fact has more strength in the key competencies than those who are not as successful. It is also crucial that work-level competencies and business-level competencies connect. While work-level competency models are often built from the bottom up, work success needs to be defined and aligned with what top-down business strategies are targeted to achieve.

Competency models often originate with the most crucial employment categories—sore points, opportunity points, or signature talent categories where companies feel it is essential to understand and leverage the elements of success. Doubletree Hotels Corporation, for example, developed a competency model for its reservation agents, in the process identifying essential competencies such as practical learning aptitude, teamwork skills, tolerance for stress and frustration, sales ability, attention to detail, and the ability to handle each call and customer on an individual basis.

The employee success profile for EMC, a Massachusetts-based manufacturer of enterprise information storage products, is built around seven categories: technical competence, goal-orientation, a sense of urgency, accountability, external and internal customer responsiveness, cross-functional behavior, and integrity.[11]

In the case of Dendrite, a New Jersey–based provider of sales force effectiveness and customer relationship management (CRM) solutions for the healthcare industry, competencies were identified and used to enhance the selection of sales and sales support professionals. As a software vendor to the pharmaceuticals industry, Dendrite screens many prospects that have pharmaceutical sales experience. Realizing that Dendrite is an IT-based business with a unique pace, culture, and productivity model, Gail Miller, Dendrite's director of recruiting, and her team utilize their talents competency model to fine-tune selection.

In an altogether different industry and for an unusual core talent category, the Cleveland Cavaliers, a team in the National Basketball Association, used a competency modeling process called Life Themes, developed by the Gallup Organization, to screen its prospective selections in the annual NBA college draft.[12] Among the essential professional basketball player competencies are court sense, ability to deal with pain, big ego (a competency in this model because of its association with the drive to compete and excel). A very different Life Themes' model, this time for the cooks and housekeepers servicing offshore oil-drilling rigs, identified competencies to be used in targeted selection aimed at reducing employee turnover. Turnover-resistant competencies here included the following: sense of order and empathy; pride and a sense of being the best at whatever they do; the ability to make others feel at home on the rig; ability to manage their own lives as well as the food supplies or cleaning materials; high-energy individuals capable of handling the physical demands and long hours involved in working offshore; and the ability to smooth out difficult situations and avoid negative thinking.

Displayed in Exhibit 6-3 is the competency model for the Frank Russell Company, a professional money management company listed among the *Fortune* 2002 best companies to work for. The model is prominently displayed on the Russell Web site career page as Behaviors Characterizing Our Values, a clear communication to current talent and talent prospects alike about the company's success factors and performance expectations.

The development of competency models, although most often prompted by recruiting needs and most directly applied in targeted selection efforts, can be extended to other talent flow processes and talent engagement processes. One of the clearest potential applications for competency model content is in prioritizing the agenda for company-wide learning.

A less immediately obvious although equally compelling reason for

Exhibit 6-3. Frank Russell Company competency model.

Behaviors Characterizing Our Values

Frank Russell Company aspires to the following behaviors in support of these values:

- Focus
- Responsiveness
- Sincere dedication to timely, quality service
- Courageous innovation: willingness to challenge conventional wisdom and methods
- Cultivation of an environment where we can learn from our mistakes and improve
- Willingness to listen
- Ability to keep perspective
- Flexibility
- Sense of humor
- Courtesy
- Confrontation with respect
- Commitment to learning
- Ability to adapt
- Celebration of the diversity of our people and their approaches
- Tolerances for the honest ambiguities of modern business life
- Management support for constructive criticism on all issues
- Clear and fearless communication

---

determining, understanding, and applying organization competencies is the collaborative impact their use can have for hiring managers and other organization leaders. For example, East Alabama Medical Center uses a targeted selection model designed and implemented with the assistance of Development Dimensions International. The trained EAMC leadership staff of 120 people conduct employment interviews using the model, where the competencies (termed *dimensions*) are adapted for talent selection from housekeeper to vice president. Use of the model makes for rigorous and stringent selection, even for nursing candidates, a talent category in huge demand nationwide, no less so in Alabama. But rigorous selection seems to pay off even here: annual percentage turnover for EAMC nurses hovers around the single digit range.

But, as we suggested, there are also internal payoffs. As EAMC's director of human resources Susan Johnston describes it, the targeted selection model gives each of the trained users a common cross-organization vocabulary to use as they team to review and screen talent prospects. "I've even had other members of the management team advise me against a selection I was ready to make for my own staff. They were right and I was wrong—and they were able to convince me based on performance dimensions we all agree are important to EAMC."[13]

Talent relationships

Companies have come to realize that it can be five to ten times more profitable to build an existing customer relationship than to try to create a new one when a customer leaves. It is the same with talent. Despite the upheaval in recruiting tactics brought about by e-cruiting, the key to the development of a predictable talent flow is having preexisting and enduring relationships that can be reliably converted into work relationships. Recognizing this, some companies are moving to a talent flow approach that mirrors the rationale of their CRM programs. The logic of talent relationship management (TRM) is that recruiting involves relationships with people who are more like customers than not.

Talent relationship management orchestrates relationships with internal and external candidates—and perhaps even with employment alumni—to create sustainable networks of talent supply into which a business can reach as positions open up or as business ventures create needs for contractors, suppliers, partners, and other talent arrangements. Talent relationship management extends the organization's branding and mind share by opening and sustaining a dialogue and moving key talent to the point where relationships can begin. Just as hires are not often made on the basis of a resume, people do not decide to join an organization based on cold call advertising. In short, TRM replaces the linear recruiting process of attracting, meeting, screening, and forgetting.

Often central to the working of a sophisticated TRM is the operation of a Web-based self-service repository of data where prospects can complete and submit profile information. These repositories are successors to the commercialized resume-storing applicant tracking systems, which first emerged in the mid-1990s. Their widespread use reflects the reality that the speed and ease of sourcing talent via e-cruiting should be matched with a capacity to store and leverage the information received.

But as essential as such technology might be, especially for larger employers with high-volume talent flow needs, technology is not the TRM differentiator. The real essence is relationships: the social network built by managers and recruiting professionals on behalf of potential employers. This has been the executive recruiting model and one of the justifications for this industry's fee structure. Now that model is moving inside, or at least closer to the company.

Relationship processes give prospects something of value well in advance of any recruitment pitch. But relationship building takes time and focus. It operates on different rhythms and thinking than the direct approach. Among the companies adopting this approach is Electronic Arts Inc., a large video game company. Electronic Arts maintains a pipeline of over thirty thousand individual relationships assembled using a Web-based ATS, which stores custom talent profiles instead of resumes. The profile data fields capture contact information, information about prospect backgrounds, career aspirations, and geographic preferences.

If prospect interests and capabilities match a current opening, the system immediately notifies the hiring manager and encourages the candidate to apply. Even for prospects whose qualifications do not make an initial match, Electronic Arts asks whether the prospect would like to receive future communications: strategic updates, information on new products, and notification of new job openings. Of the people registered in the database, some twenty thousand have answered yes to that option.[14]

A larger-scale TRM example is Prudential Financial. Prudential, in Newark, New Jersey, is one of the largest financial services institutions in the United States, providing insurance, investment management, and other financial products and services to over 15 million individual and institutional customers.

To help supply its substantial long-term talent acquisition needs, Prudential has for years used and maintained a traditional ATS. Yet, Mike Lowe, Prudential's vice president of global talent acquisition, grew concerned that this talent inventorying approach was more reactive than proactive. For example, even with new Web interface capabilities, ATS use had become overly focused on record keeping and reporting. Although job applicants could submit resumes electronically (for ATS storage) in response to specific current employment needs displayed on Prudential's Web site or on commercial job boards, this need-response model did not permit the fostering of relationships that could enhance Prudential's employer brand as well as support its ongoing long-term talent needs. The need was for a more robust solution, reflecting Prudential's Internet presence and its emergence as a publicly traded financial services company.

The solution, now prominent on Prudential's Web-based employment center, is the opportunity for visitors to quickly initiate and establish a relationship with Prudential. Visitors are asked to register—anonymously or by name—by providing menu-based answers to eleven questions (criteria boxes) on job preferences, experience, and education. Once registered, visitors have ongoing options to make online submissions for openings and to receive e-mail notification of matching opportunities. More important, both for Prudential and registrants, is that registrants assume a measure of control over their relationship with the company.

Becky Perez, Prudential's director of sourcing, manages the solution and the relationship with Prudential's TRM vendor Hire.com whose technology tools enable the process. Since its launch in January 2001, the initiative has captured approximately one hundred thirty thousand profiles, according to Perez, roughly ten times the resume-based traffic that would otherwise have been deposited in the ATS. Physical data entry or resume scanning has been reduced by 80 percent; recruiting cycle time has been decreased 20 percent; and resorting to external searches has been reduced several (hard-dollar substantial) percentage points.

More importantly, with the integration of other talent flow process elements such as job requisitioning, job posting, commercial job boards, and employee referral programs, Prudential's talent branding and acquisition strategies are now able to center around its Web presence— where company and employment information can be reliably communicated and where prospect interest can be efficiently captured.

Along with other financial companies, Prudential Financial has experienced some of the downsizing realities of the financial services industry. The employee referral module of its talent relationship system, for example, was launched immediately prior to the tragic events of September 11, 2001, and their impact on the financial services industry. Yet, even during a period when it may not be aggressively recruiting, Prudential's corporate recruiting team must continue to scout for talent with security firm experience (taking advantage, for example, of the financial service talent community's new interest in employment opportunities with blue chip companies located near but outside of Manhattan's downtown financial district). Prudential's talent relationship capabilities provide it with the ongoing capability to establish and nurture relationships during periods when talent spotting can be most fruitful.

Of course, initiating these relationships is one thing. The real value is in how actively the relationships are developed and pursued. For example, Electronic Arts has used its relationship base for the digital marketing of employment opportunities. To jumpstart talent acquisition for the opening of a new development studio in Orlando, Florida, EA sent interactive e-mails to about eighteen thousand contacts. Dramatic preview clips of the computer games to be developed at the new studio accompanied the e-mails. In similar fashion, Prudential has the capability to conduct digital talent market research as it considers the talent implications of opening new facilities or transferring current facilities.

Talent relationship management need not always involve extensive system investments—companies can also engage in successful low-tech/high-touch TRM. Often this involves direct TRM involvement by hiring managers whose participation typically adds value beyond talent acquisition. The process of developing talent relationships forces managers to develop a more outward-looking view; stay on top of cutting-edge trends; build their company's image; and learn the latest trends, products, employee, and customer expectations. Hiring manager involvement ensures that the knowledge acquired in the recruiting process is not lost.

For example, Electronic Arts maintains a top forty list of the most-talented people throughout the world who, the company hopes, will someday work with them. As part of their business travel itineraries, Electronic Arts executives make a point of contacting and meeting with people from the list. In similar fashion, Lynda Welch, director of recruiting for Lockheed Martin Information Management Services (now ACS State and Local Solutions) in Teaneck, New Jersey, has collaborated with managers across her organization in identifying and establishing relationships with key external talent prospects targeted for new ventures.

In sum, preemployment relationships (and postemployment alumni relationships) give employers the capability to mix and match recruiting and staffing information to better match real-time talent needs with real-time talent availability. This is done easily enough in an employment buyer's market. But in a seller's market, having a reserve of established relationships also enables the unbundling and rearrangement of work—the traditional job may need to be fractured, but getting the work accomplished does not.

Retaining talent

In the aftermath of World War II, the U.S. military asked Harvard historian S.L.A. Marshall to research a fundamental question essential to the strategy of conflict: Why were men willing to sacrifice their lives in battle? Marshall tested a range of explanations, among them patriotism—people would die for their country—or family—men would fight and die to protect their wives and children. The answer that finally emerged from the study was fundamental: small-group integrity. In basic terms, the feeling of being part of a group that is truly committed to its members enables most people to withstand the effects of fear and imminent danger: You don't want to be the first to run, so you all stand and fight together.

While such organizational commitment and involvement is clearly the extreme, Marshall's findings nonetheless reflect both the dilemmas and opportunities that employers face when they consider employee retention/turnover in the context of business and talent strategies.

Employee turnover has for a long time been judged as a barometer of issues such as employee satisfaction, morale, and motivation. Organizations expect some level of turnover, although norms for combined voluntary and involuntary turnover, expressed usually as an annual percentage of the employer workforce, can vary widely, from under 5 percent to high triple-digit percentages (in retail or in low skill-manufacturing environments). The past few years gave ample evidence of the direction and momentum of the concept of employee loyalty. According to reports from the California-based Saratoga Institute, turnover rates at U.S. companies have increased by nearly 20 percent during the past five years, to an average annual rate of 16.5 percent. At European companies, employee turnover was up by 10 percent in 1999, to an average of 14 percent, according to Saratoga Europe. Attrition during the first year of employment—always greater than rates thereafter—has soared to an average annual rate nearing 30 percent. (Specific turnover rates as reported for some industries and professions are shown in Exhibit 6-4.)[15]

Having much more than the expected level is usually symptomatic of internal problems and unnecessary costs that needed to be pinpointed and managed. (See Chapter 8 for calculating the costs of turnover.) At the height and near the end of the most recent talent wars, organizations devoted increasing attention to the causes and costs of attrition. Many companies that were struggling to source and find new employees ultimately realized that these efforts to get people in via the front door made little headway if a competing number of both recent hires and longer-term employees bailed out (or were poached out) the back. Even organizations that had succeeded with their employment objectives gained a new awareness of the cost, invested time, performance value, and the lure of the market for the talent they had acquired.

Exhibit 6-4. Turnover rates.

Turnover rates

- The national turnover rates according to the **National Association for Health Care Recruitment** are 18.1 percent overall and **15.2 percent for RNs.**

- **15.6%:** U.S. National Median Value from Bureau of National Affairs Inc, Washington, D.C., second quarter 2000 permanent separation.

- The average annual turnover for the 88 stores studied was **204 percent,** with turnover **ranging from 31 percent in one store to 390** in another.
  SOURCE: *"The Relationship Between Imminent Turnover and Employee Theft," research study of turnover and theft at one of the largest **fast-food restaurant chain**s in the country by Paula Wolper, Kimberly S. Scott, Dave Jones*

- Turnover rates for California PWB **printed wiring board manufacturers** average **8% for exempt** and **17% for non-exempt** employees.
  SOURCE: *April 1998 membership survey by the California Circuits Association (CCA)*

- **21.8 percent** turnover in **business and professional services** is the highest rate outside of **wholesale and retail's 32.6 percent.** The rate for **all industries** was **16.9 percent**
  SOURCE: *AMA mid-2000 annual survey (1,192 respondents)*

- Individuals who exited **Transportation,** represent **14.9 percent** of the total
  SOURCE: *2001 study by the Wyoming Department of Employment, Research & Planning*

Marshall's research makes the point that retention can be affected by unexpected and intrinsic factors. Although choosing to belong or continuing to belong to a work organization hardly requires the agonizing choices and commitments revealed in Marshall's study of wartime courage, some of the same psychology seems to be relevant in understanding talent retention, and its flipside, turnover.

Underlying many employer retention efforts is the expectation that finding the correct combination of compensation programs, career paths, job content, training efforts, and similar workplace variables can insulate employers from damaging turnover. The problem is that for some workplace factors much tinkering will need to be done to make an impact. (Recall the Ford Motor example cited in Chapter 3: a doubling of daily pay to five dollars reduced turnover by 85 percent.) And some supposedly crucial factors may show up on the radar of talent policy makers while hardly registering with key talent. On the other hand, a retention-at-all-costs approach, even if it delivers the numbers, can also contradict business strategy objectives. (Imagine here the United States trying to keep its postwar armed forces when the country could make other, better uses of its resources and soldiers could make other, better uses of their time and skills.)

While retention of key talent may be a fundamental component of a comprehensive talent strategy plan, that component shouldn't be based on trying to single-handedly reconstruct demolished assumptions of employee loyalty and long-term commitment or on a line-in-the-sand conviction that all turnover is damaging turnover. Retention initiatives must take into account the logic of the talent marketplace where the market, not the employer, will more often have a disproportionate impact on employee turnover. Accepting this reality, companies can adopt a broader view. Turnover is an inevitable part of talent flow. Although it cannot be stopped, it can be channeled into a balance of desired retention and acceptable turnover. Retention does not mean only the preservation of the status quo in a working relationship. Rather, it is more a matter of maintaining goodwill in business relationships as they evolve through changing circumstances.

Factors that influence retention

The reasons for turnover, although more market driven than before, still involve factors that extend from the economy to the individual (see Exhibit 6-5). The economy and industry factors, for example, always influence turnover. Economic and industry conditions determine overall employment opportunities. In a tight economy with fewer opportuni-

Exhibit 6-5. Retention/turnover impact.

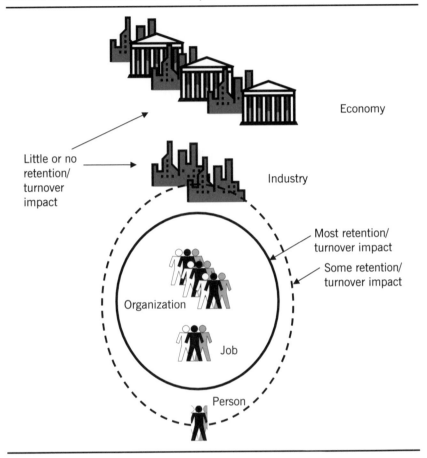

ties, employees are less willing to leave their current jobs whatever their level of commitment.

Industry trends sometimes drive or mirror general economic trends. For example, the high-tech industry continues to fuel a significant portion of the wider economy. High tech puts a premium on knowledge workers with current training—enhancing opportunities for recent graduates and temporary contractors while reducing opportunities for older workers and limiting creation of lower wage jobs. In this way, industry characteristics influence workforce composition—for high tech, a workforce of younger (higher turnover), transient workers with skills that command competitive bidding. Employers respond by paying premiums to key employees or by revamping employment relationships; for example, using contractors for specific projects or time periods.

At the next level within organizations, there are a few fundamental workforce demographics that influence turnover despite economy/industry trends or company talent strategy initiatives, for example:

- A younger workforce will change jobs and employers more than will an older workforce.
- Workforces weighted toward part-time talent are less stable than workforces weighted to full-time talent.
- Retention generates retention: Workforces with greater average tenure will have fewer turnovers than workforces with less average tenure.

Beyond these basic demographics, there is a set of organization factors that seem able to leverage workforce turnover and retention, such as:

- *Company image.* Positive business and community image seems to strongly affect turnover and retention. For example, a cross-cultural study by the Society of Personality and Social Psychology indicated that the best indicator of turnover in both Britain and Japan was lack of identification with the employing organization. A 2001 study conducted by the University of Southern California's (USC) Center for Effective Organizations reports similar cross-cultural results and points to the origins of employer identification: Employee retention is influenced by identification with the company; and employees identify more closely with the company if they believe it has a viable and well-communicated strategy for success.

- *Recruiting, selection, and deployment.* A large share of turnover outcomes is ordained by the quality and rigor of talent flow processes that precede them.

- *Leadership*. One apparently enduring reality is that employees join companies and leave managers. Leadership problems are frequently associated with turnover. Conflicts with immediate supervisors are often mentioned in exit interviews.

- *Learning*. The emphasis an organization places on developing the skills of its employees has an impact on turnover. A survey of one thousand companies with fifty or more employees conducted by the U.S. Department of Labor's Bureau of Labor Statistics found a negative correlation between company turnover and its level of training expenditure. Companies with low turnover rates spent more than twice what those with high turnover rates spent.

- *Performance recognition and rewards*. Pay dissatisfaction is usually the first reason people think of for leaving a job. However, pay may be cited as a departure reason in exit interviews when other causes are present, which people are reluctant to discuss as candidly. Nevertheless, in competitive labor markets, pay certainly matters.

At the level of the individual, demographic, intrinsic, and situational factors influence turnover. The USC study indicates the following demographic influences:

- For early career employees—those age 30 and under—career advancement is very significant to retention.
- For mid-career employees—those age 31 to 50—ability to manage career and professional satisfaction influence retention.
- For late career employees—those over age 50—job security drives retention.

As examples of intrinsic and situational factors, risk-adverse individuals with higher needs for security are generally less likely to leave, as are individuals with local ties or financial dependencies.

Good turnover, bad turnover

Not all turnover is equal. A fundamental step for incorporating retention/turnover issues in talent strategies is understanding different turnover segments: some desirable, some not; some controllable, some not (see Exhibit 6-6):

- *Undesirable, controllable.* Good employees leave for reasons that the company could have done something about.
- *Undesirable, uncontrollable.* Good employees leave for reasons beyond the employer's control; for example, because of individual factors such as a relocated spouse.
- *Desirable, controllable.* Poor employees leave through dismissal or performance-based restructuring.
- *Desirable, uncontrollable.* Poor employees leave for their own reasons.

All types of turnover involve replacement costs—assuming, of course, there are replacements to be made. Indeed, much turnover (usually 50 percent or more) occurs within the first six months of employment where the bulk of costs are replacement costs. That being said, undesirable turnover typically incurs costs that are greater than simple

Exhibit 6-6. Workforce turnover matrix.

Controllable	Bad Turnover	Good Turnover
	Key role ★	Key role
	Good performer ★	Good performer
	Could have retained ★	Could have retained ★
	Unfortunate Turnover	Good Turnover
Uncontrollable	Key role ★	Key role
	Good performer ★	Good performer
	Could have retained	Could have retained
	Undesirable	Desirable

replacement costs. These costs increase with factors such as employment length, work contribution, the value lost in knowledge, and investments made in employee development. We'll explore the scope and magnitude of these costs in more detail in Chapter 8.

Turnover cycle, turnover duration

Two other retention/turnover dynamics deserve mention. When employers in industries such as retail or food service experience annual turnover rates well approaching or exceeding 100 percent, it doesn't mean the hiring and departure of an entire workforce during a year. Instead, it usually means that low-paying, entry-level positions are experiencing constant, almost phenomenal turnover—there are many cycles of hiring, training, departure, and replacement. Even though, at least in a slow economy, replacements may be found easily and quickly, the constant drain of training investment and administrative transactions can be costly and disruptive.

At the other end of the spectrum, even low turnover can be disproportionately painful to an organization. For example, if some management or professional positions rarely fall vacant but, when they do, the organization has extreme difficulty in finding qualified replacements, this can quickly and justifiably be perceived as unacceptable turnover. Unacceptable, because what is at stake are substantial revenue or business opportunity costs. And the same can be true for professional and technical positions where departures may be relatively few but occur in a job area that is expanding.

In 1990 and 1991 the U.S. Department of Labor conducted a study of employee turnover and job openings in the following eight industries: oil and gas extraction; special trade contractors; electronic and other electrical equipment; trucking, warehousing, and machinery; equipment and supplies wholesaling; eating and drinking places; depository institutions; and hospitals.[16] Because of the labor intensity of these industries, the data reflect turnover trends involving thousands of employee departures and replacements across major occupational categories in hundreds of companies. Looking at one slice of the data (see Exhibit

6-7) illustrates the patterns of high turnover/easy replacement and low turnover/difficult replacement scenarios. Recognizing that researchers collected this multiemployer data in the midst of the 1990 to 1991 recession (the most recent economic downturn before 2001), gives some sense of the numbers, costs, and psychological impact of turnover during the height of the most recent talent war.

Building retention into talent flow strategies

Why talent leaves, then, is at least as complicated as why talent joins. The answer involves the economy, the industry, the company, the job, and the individual. Some turnover is desirable, while some is not; some turnover can be controlled, and some cannot. Retention initiatives must consider these variables, anticipate outcomes, react but not over-react.

Most successful retention efforts we encounter are not retention initiatives per se. They are talent flow or engagement initiatives whose payoffs include improved retention, although not exclusively. That being said, when companies direct attention to retention, there can be noticeable payoffs. For example, according to the 2002 Hackett Best Practices study of best practices in human resources, companies that have formal employee retention plans in place have two-year retention rates that are 17 percent better than at average companies and turnover costs that are 31 percent lower.

One classic, often-cited example is that of SAS Institute Inc., a statistical analysis software company based in Cary, North Carolina. Annual turnover at SAS, a private company, has purportedly never exceeded 5 percent, and in one year was reported at 3.7 percent.[17] SAS has what only could be described as a lavish array of employee benefits, employee services, and work/life balancing initiatives. A partial listing (compiled in 1999) includes a thirty-five-hour full-time workweek; unlimited soda, coffee, tea, and juice; two on-site day-care facilities and one off-site facility; an on-site health clinic staffed with six nurse practitioners and two physicians; no-cost health insurance for employees; unlimited sick days; and a 36,000-square-foot on-site gym. One rationale for the amenities is

Exhibit 6-7. High turnover/easy replacement; low turnover/difficult replacement.

(a) Occupation	(b) Separations*	(c) New hires*	(d) Job openings*	(e) Proportion of jobs open more than four weeks (%)	(f) Ratio of new hires to job openings
Managerial	21	15	18	63.6	.83
Professional and technical	40	40	97	60.7	.41
Sales	56	66	9	24.7	7.00
Service	317	351	141	11.0	2.49

*Numbers in thousands

- Column **(a)** shows the broad occupational categories.
- Column **(b)** shows separations during a three-month period.
- Turnover for managers, professionals, and technicals represents a small proportion—roughly 14%. The substantial balance of separation occurs among sales and service workers.
- For managers, new hires (column **(c)**) lag behind both separations and end of period job openings (column **(d)**). Further, the proportion of managerial jobs still open after four weeks (column **(e)**) is high—in this case 63.6%.
- Column **(f)** results (column **(c)** divided by column **(d)**) of .83 show hires lagging vacancies. The key number here is the proportion of vacancies with long duration in the midst of otherwise low turnover.
- For professional and technical occupations, while new hires keep pace with separations, employers are losing ground in these occupations.
- Substantial growth in demand for professional and technical talent is reflected in column **(d)**; a high proportion (nearly 61%) of jobs remain open after 4 weeks; there is a low ratio (.41) of new hires to end of period job openings. Relatively low turnover is happening against a headwind of burgeoning talent demand.
- For sales and service occupations there are more separations, reflecting the greater talent populations. The proportion of jobs open after four weeks is dramatically lower than proportions for managerial, professional, and technical occupations (about 25% for sales talent, 11% for service talent).
- New sales and service hires exceed separations and there is the high ratio of new hires to end of period job openings. Jobs are getting filled quickly in constantly repeating cycles of departure and new hiring.
- While per transaction costs for sales and service may be low, the separation volume makes them high and the separation frequently makes it difficult to recoup investment.

Source: Richard M. Devins, Jr., "The Employee Turnover and Job Openings Survey," *Monthly Labor Review,* March 1992.

that having access to them makes it impossible for people not to do their work. More fundamentally, the SAS approach does build in some remunerative trade-offs: salaries, for example, are no better than competitive; and, as a private company, it offers no stock. However, the biggest trade-off, intentional or not, seems to be on turnover. With annual turnover savings estimated to be in the $60 million range, the amenities are judged to be cost-accountable.[18]

Closer to earth, one or more talent strategy initiatives of companies we interviewed seemed to have a less direct, but certainly noticeable impact on retention; although, again, this may not have been their origin. For example, EAMC's use of a rigorous competency-based selection model to minimize bad hiring actions, combined with a total rewards program that incorporates twice yearly cash gainsharing payments (described in Chapter 7), favorably influences overall turnover, and helps to keep annual turnover in the crucial nursing category in the single digits. For The Container Store, a combination of rigorous screening, substantial commitment to employee learning (235 hours annually), and unusually competitive salaries for the retail environment seems to have a similar impact in an industry segment where turnover is endemic: annual turnover of 28 percent for its full-time salespeople versus an industry average of 73.6 percent; and just 5.3 percent of its store managers, compared with the industry average of 33.6 percent.

Despite these signature successes, a fundamental reality remains: The people you wish would stay are the ones most likely to leave. And they'll leave because they can leave—they simply have more marketplace options. The marketplace, which includes search firms and job boards (Monster.com has 15 million resumes in its database), is apt to know more about a company's workforce than the company itself. People leave their companies when the cost of staying exceeds the reward of leaving. Thus, retention initiatives involve a certain amount of triage:

- Who are the company's wealth creators?
- What is the impact of their turnover?

- What cost-effective efforts can you reasonably make to control their turnover?

Consider a simple example that hinges on the turnover behavior of a company's wealth creators—the vital subset of employees in specific jobs, professions, or high-impact settings whose work results or products drive business strategy and revenue. They might be product designers or software architects or machinists or business analysts. Whatever the context, the turnover behavior of these individuals has a disproportionate impact on the business. For the example shown in Exhibit 6-8, a relatively small organization of one thousand people has a group of fifty key employees. Voluntary departures for this business during one year were two hundred, divided between key employee and non-key employee departures. This simple example reveals the point. What seems, on a company-wide basis, to be hardly a crisis situation, becomes one when looked at on a segmented basis.

Successful talent retention strategies, then, need to strike a balance between addressing organizational turnover factors and individual factors. They are not one-size-fits-all solutions. At the organization level, having a good, clearly communicated business strategy, which people understand and can get behind, seems to be a strong retention tool. Signature talent strategies that foster group integrity also seem to be key, such as EAMC's gain-sharing program or The Container Store's focus on learning. At the individual level, strategy initiatives should hone in on controllable/undesirable turnover risks, and on a case-by-case basis.

Exhibit 6-8. Turnover example.

	# Employees	Voluntary departures	Turnover %
Key employees	50	25	50%
Non-key employees	950	175	18%
Combined	1,000	200	20%

Alumni relationships

Michael R. Bloomberg, founder and CEO of Bloomberg L.P., an information services, news, and media company—and currently mayor of New York City—is straightforward, unbending, and notorious on the matter of former employees. They do not exist. An employee's decision to leave Bloomberg is an irrevocable decision and the employee is automatically ineligible for reemployment. The policy has been a cornerstone of Bloomberg's talent value proposition, one that focuses on competition and a tightly knit circle of an organization. Leaving employment is leaving the circle forever.

Approaches to reemployment vary widely across the employer landscape, although Bloomberg's is probably at the far, uncompromising end of the spectrum. Some organizations are either explicitly (like Bloomberg) or quietly adamant that departed employees not return. Other employers are vague. They may allow rehires—often called boomerangs—on paper, but discourage it in practice. The real issue here is how does such a policy fit in with business strategy? How does it fit with the realities of the skills and expertise that a business needs? What flexibility does it add? If you forever subtract from the total talent pool available to you the skills and contributions of people who have worked for you previously, especially those who worked effectively and departed on good terms, what are the consequences? Bloomberg's conclusion seems to be that reemployment is counter to strategy. But what about other strategy circumstances?

Many companies feel quite differently. To these companies former employees are the ultimate untapped resource, deserving of ongoing engagement rather than a somber escort to the lobby, a box of possessions in tow: Former employees move on to become clients (studies have shown that 20 to 50 percent of exiting employees move on to work for clients or potential clients) and sources of referrals (some leading-edge companies have even expanded their current referral bonus programs to their former employees). They also become potential future employees experienced in the business, familiar with the culture, and perhaps also trained and developed at someone else's expense. A comparatively short initial employee relationship is leveraged as a potentially enduring human capital investment.

Of course, this is not a new concept. Universities have long used these alumni relations' strategies. By promoting the university experience as a lifelong benefit, universities reap the benefits of annual giving and endowment fund-raising, and are able to leverage their brand through the accomplishments and recommendations of their graduates.

Now, a range of other companies are either sampling or embracing this approach, not for all former employees of course, but for ones who have potential for future value and contribution. One Monster.com survey about employers' willingness to accept so-called boomerang employees found 71 percent of employers willing to rehire former employees, albeit cautiously. Another 21 percent indicated an open-arms approach, because of recruitment savings in time and money. But there are other rationales as well:

- The company's investment in the knowledge and expertise of a valued employee who leaves should not be routinely marked down to zero. Former employees represent intellectual capital. Continuing the relationships allows companies to remain tapped into valuable knowledge.

- Through their experience with customer relationship management processes companies understand that, much as it is with customers, it is often more productive to invest time in cultivating relationships you already have—even when they are dormant—than it is to constantly scour for new relationships.

- Many exits have to do with business cycles. In the advertising industry, for example, accounts change, clients change, and companies change agencies—circumstances that employees cannot be held accountable for. For these reasons an advertising firm such as J. Walter Thompson, which already averages between five and seven rehires a quarter for its North American operations, extends the process to a formal Web-enabled alumni network. The process and infrastructure includes job postings and channels for alumni to refer potential hires to fill opportunities. Ultimately the network will include a searchable database of former JWT employees with current information on work locations and skills.

• Other employment exits often have to do with personal and career circumstances that cannot be accommodated by the employer at the time (for example, promotional opportunities, a chance to work with certain technologies, the relocation of a spouse) but can be resolved in another setting. Rehires return having had the opportunity to sample other experiences—perhaps to get them out of their systems—and come back with higher levels of commitment and a stabilizing influence. For Gensler, a global architecture, design, and planning company, this rationale has translated to rehires representing 12 percent of its annual U.S. hires. Former employees who return to Gensler now even get an official company boomerang.[19]

• The move to another employer may fill out the white spaces in a key employee's skills, experiences, or relationships, making them newly strong employment candidates. Using this rationale, the Warren, New Jersey–based Chubb Group of Insurance Companies makes it a practice to include former employees in lists of prospects received by hiring managers during the recruitment process. A once informal process has become more targeted, particularly when hiring for a challenging position. The company goes back about three years when identifying former high-performance employees to be considered. Roughly 10 percent of all hires are rehires at Chubb, with rehires occurring across all the company's levels and geographic areas.

• Reemployment need not be a return to traditional employment. Alumni networks also can prove essential for identifying former employees who can add their knowledge and expertise either on a contract or freelance basis.

For these and other reasons, many employers that may have occasionally accommodated these situations are being more formal and purposeful in managing them.

Two new alumni relationship variations have emerged in the recent downturn. One variation, called assimilation consulting, provides downsized senior executives with several months of counseling—at their former employer's expense—on successfully settling into a new job.[20] Why would an employer go this far for people it no longer wants? The motivation of some employers using this outplacement approach is to do everything possible to see that their former employees end up happy—and thus less likely to sue.

But for Charles Schwab Corp., the motivation seems to reflect a view to the future. Schwab included ninety days of assimilation coaching in its outplacement package for two thousand employees it laid off with the hope that, combined with a $7,500 bonus for anyone rehired over the next eighteen months, the assimilation benefit will keep allegiance to Schwab alive—and will increase rehiring prospects for the future.

Schwab, along with other companies like Cisco, Texas Instruments, and Accenture, is also trying a twenty-first-century version of the old industrial furlough, in effect "parking" employees until the economy recovers. Cisco, in its pilot program, paid seventy employees one-third of their salaries while lending them to nonprofit organizations for a year.[21]

Notes

1. Keith H. Hammonds, "Michael Porter's Big Ideas," *Fast Company* 44, March 2001, p.150.

2. According to a recent report from investment firm Goldman Sachs, revenues from business-process outsourcing, a fragmented but huge combination of information-technology related products and services, could grow to between $300 billion and $500 billion by 2004.

3. SHRM®/Fisher College HR Strategies, Stages of Development and Organization Size Survey.

4. Cheryl Dahle, "Big Learning, Fast Futures," *Fast Company*, June 1999, p. 46.

5. Saul Hansell, "The Monster That's Feasting on Newspapers," *The New York Times*, March 24, 2002, section 3, p. 1.

6. Industry demographic data on search and corporate recruiting from *Recruiter Magazine*.

7. Comparing the macro to the micro is risky at best, but consider this: combining the annual U.S. recruiting figures—$6.4 billion in recruitment advertisements, the $115 billion in search revenues, and the $25.5 billion in recruiting infrastructure—gives us a total of about $147 billion. The U.S. 2000 workforce population was 145 million. Assuming a turnover rate of 16.5% annually (based on data from the Saratoga Institute), or 23.9 million, the $147 billion translates to a cost per hire of about $615.

8. The survey compares cost-per-hire (CPH) and recruiting efficiency measures for 679 responding organizations covering nearly 905,000 hiring actions. See Chapter 8 for additional details.

9. Using the alternative staffing efficiency measure, small-/medium-size company hiring processes are 25 percent less efficient. However, a qualitative, strategic view may suggest another and very plausible explanation: that small company hires are disproportionately crucial and impactive—requiring more time and more internal screening scrutiny.

10. Peter F. Drucker, "The Information Executives Truly Need," *Harvard Business Review on Measuring Corporate Performance* (Boston: Harvard Business School Press, 1998), p. 17.

11. Bill Birchard, "Hire Great People Fast," *Fast Company*, August 1997, p. 132.

12. Len Schlesinger, "The Theory Behind Life Themes," *Fast Company*, November 1993, p. 87.

13. Interview with Susan Johnston, 2002.

14. Anna Muoio, "Man with a Talent Plan," *Fast Company*, January 2001, p. 83.

15. Trying to compare turnover figures across markets or across industries is risky. This is really an apples and oranges situation. One industry's acceptable level of turnover—anything less than 100 percent in certain retail categories, for example—would spell talent disaster for most others.

16. Richard M. Devins, Jr. "The Employee Turnover and Job Openings Survey," *Monthly Labor Review*, March 1992, p. 29.

17. Charles Fishman, "Sanity Inc.," *Fast Company*, January 1999, p. 85.

18. Ibid., p. 85.

19. Scott Kirsner, "Hire Today Gone Tomorrow?" *Fast Company*, August 1998, p. 136.

20. Pamela Mendels, "Gone but Not Forgotten," *Business Week Online*, May 22, 2001.

21. Louis Uchitelle, "As Job Cuts Spread, Tears Replace Anger," *The New York Times*, August 5, 2001, section 3, p. 1.

CHAPTER 7

◪ TALENT ENGAGEMENT STRATEGIES

More than "being there"

*B*EING THERE, A NOVEL AND movie from the 1970s, tells the story of Chauncey Gardiner, a mysterious but apparently distinguished man who emerges literally from nowhere to become a Wall Street tycoon and presidential policy adviser. It is hard to figure out what Chauncey has actually done to earn either his wealth or reputation. Everyone quotes Chauncey, although no one really understands what he is talking about. That is because Chauncey, it turns out, really *is* a gardener whose accidental position and prestige have nothing to do with his abilities and everything to do with just being there.

Just "being there" describes some of the more redundant features of the traditional employment model. Just-in-case workforces, based on locking in talent, do not necessarily translate to the best leveraging of talent—either to support business strategies or for the career growth of people. The talent architecture of this model often had people queuing up in anticipation of internal career opportunities. While waiting, they would likely receive company-specific or function-specific training; they might receive a supervisor's appraisal of their performance; and they could expect annual pay adjustments based nominally—but not usually directly—on job performance.

The routine predictability of this model has been disrupted by the employment and business marketplace upheavals of recent years. With more fluid talent flow have come new, sometimes aggressive expectations—on the talent side and on the employer side—about how work performance should be structured, informed, evaluated, and rewarded.

Talent engagement processes

What is often captured under the umbrella term *development* we term *engagement*; we use it both to describe what should be occurring and what we believe successful talent strategies achieve. Engagement is about maximizing the value of people in a mutually rewarding work relationship. We feel engagement better describes the immediacy of the new work model—from the employer side, in terms of productive contributions, and from the talent side, in terms of accomplishment and career security.

In this chapter we cover four engagement issues. The first is the crucial transition from talent flow to talent engagement. The second is performance management, a concept/process that is often the odd one out when it comes to talent strategies. Third is the issue of organization learning, and fourth is the issue of rewards.

Talent flow to talent engagement

Talent flow processes can only achieve so much. Successful recruiting and relationship processes deliver talented people. Indeed, a company can lose the business game by not acquiring the right talent. But success-ful talent strategies hinge as much, or more, on what a company does once it has good people.[1]

Talent flow and talent engagement processes overlap. It is impor-tant for engaging performance to get off to the right start at the juncture where offer, closing, and hiring converge on employment. Unfortu-nately, during this handoff many employers routinely drop the ball. *Ori-entation* is often the term used to describe this handoff—intentionally or unintentionally implying that talent arrives dazed, confused, and unpre-pared. If this is the expectation, then orientation does not improve the situation if it comes late, covers only surface logistics, or never happens at all. This scenario leaves newly arrived talent in limbo, left to wonder when, where, and how they're supposed to fit into the organization's plans—and perhaps clueless about what those plans include. Under life-time employment arrangements, lapses here may not have mattered much in the overall scheme of things. There was downtime enough to catch up and get filled in. Now, with time-to-productivity a pressing concern for both employer and talent—that grace time often no longer exists.

Depending on what happens at the intersection of flow and engage-ment, some key trends are set: Talent either learns or it doesn't about business strategies, objectives, and processes. The logistics are in place—or are lacking—to speed productivity. The courting relationship moves smoothly into the employment relationship, which in turn fits somehow into what the business is trying to achieve—or all three rela-tionships risk failure.

Talent strategy initiatives that succeed in this transition accomplish two things: They allow new talent to hit the ground running by rou-tinely anticipating and handling workplace logistics and they front-load talent's exposure to business strategies, business issues, and essential work processes.

Cisco Systems is a prime example of a company that has learned to make the most of the segue from talent flow to talent engagement. In 1997, in the wake of survey results indicating that newly arrived talent felt more like baggage than assets, Cisco launched a series of new employee orientation initiatives collectively called Fast Start.[2] Prior to new employee arrivals, facility teams are alerted to arrange the logistics of workspace, telephone, computer, e-mail, and initial software training. When new employees arrive, essential support systems are already up and running. They get two days of training in Cisco business essentials, covering company history, the networking market, and Cisco's business units. Two weeks after new hires start, their managers are prompted by e-mail to review departmental initiatives and personal goals with them. Finally, a "buddy" (peer sponsor) is assigned to ease the way for every new employee.

The Container Store is another example, this time with top-level guidance and store-level followthrough. Its foundation principles, mentioned in Chapter 6 as integral to the company's talent value proposition, also serve as a concise guidebook for linking new talent efforts to business strategies. New Container Store talent are told they should trust their instincts as long as their actions follow the six principles. And principles are also supplemented by intense in store training—an average of 235 hours each year—guided by a trainer assigned to each of the store's twenty outlets.

Performance management

An organization's best people can have an outsized impact on that organization's success. Certainly, they have an impact on levels of productivity and work performance. But just how substantial and valuable an impact is often missed. For example, when managers are asked to estimate the difference between the productivity of the worst worker and most productive worker, they often estimate a magnitude of difference somewhere between five and ten times. Yet, looking at jobs where productivity is easily measured, such as the amount of error-free code produced by computer programmers, the best performers have been shown to be over twenty times more effective than average performers. Now consider how much the best employee is or should be paid versus the worst employee. The frequent response here is about 10 percent to 15 percent more. In other words, actual performance differences may be orders of magnitude bigger than supposedly commensurate pay differences.

Companies have always struggled with the meaning and implications of performance differences, measurement, and management. Among the recurring questions are: Is performance measurement for feedback purposes only? Should it focus on the past or the future? How should it be linked to pay? What should the upside be for good performance, or the consequence for poor? In practice, the term *performance management* often ends up being a semantic label for the thorny issue of individually evaluating and appraising talent performance. It is a process where the appraiser is often reluctant about providing forthright feedback and the recipient is often nervous, cynical, or both about receiving it. Under lifetime employment arrangements, it was easy for either side to downplay the importance of performance management and go through the motions—or even to avoid the motions. There was often limited upside for great performance and limited downside for average or even substandard performance.

The low opinion of many companies about performance management rituals is no secret. In a 1995 polling by consulting firm William M. Mercer Inc, for example, only 7 percent of executives said their companies' performance management processes were excellent, and more than 70 percent said they had revamped them or were planning to. Similar sentiments were evident two years later in a study jointly sponsored by the Society for Human Resources Management (SHRM) and Aon Consulting. In this study, only 5 percent of HR professionals reported being "very satisfied" with their companies' performance management processes.[3]

Not surprisingly, during the height of the talent wars, performance management's stock went still lower. The desperation of many companies to find and hold talent created a "kind of corporate Lake Wobegon, in which all performances were strong and all cube dwellers above average."[4] A sample of anecdotes suggests the mood: Powertrain Group, a GM subsidiary, became so fed up with traditional reviews that it abolished them. Glenroy Inc., a Wisconsin-based manufacturer of packaging materials, held a rally in the company parking lot where employees stoked a bonfire with company policy manuals; Glenroy's performance review process literally went up in smoke, never to be reinstated. Parkview Medical Center in Pueblo, Colorado, replaced top-down appraisals with a feel-good Annual Piece of Paper (APOP) program consisting of bottom-up requests for assistance.[5]

More recent trends, however, point to a resurgence in the relevance and impact of performance management. One of these trends is on the talent side: Where people used to focus on building careers across jobs, they now build careers across jobs, across employers, and across a varied portfolio of experiences and settings—projects, contracts, teams, special assignments, and competencies. They have an increased personal stake in their talent market value: They want to understand what is expected of them, how it will be measured, how it contributes to what comes next, and what they will get for a job done well. What they will get, of course, implies near-term financial rewards, but it also may be having their achievements documented, acknowledged, and accredited. For example, in a survey of MBA students worldwide conducted by PricewaterhouseCoopers, students said what they wanted most out of their first job was to obtain a good reference for their future career.

Perhaps because of this, performance management's reputation and potential also seems to be making something of a comeback among companies. For example, results from a 2000 study jointly sponsored by SHRM and Personnel Decisions Incorporated, a Minneapolis-headquartered consulting firm, were favorable: 61 percent said they were satisfied or very satisfied with performance management at their companies.[6]

At the same time, many respondents expressed disappointment over the gap between what they thought performance management should achieve and what it actually achieves. Although most felt the primary objective should be information sharing with employees, only one in three expressed satisfaction with how this information sharing actually gets translated into talent development: Relatively few reported that specific development plans were in place, either for company executives (25 percent), midlevel employees (17 percent), or nonexempts (12 percent). Similar gaps were seen in the links between performance goals and business outcomes. Although most (75 percent) reported that company executives had performance goals linked to operating results, far fewer (36 percent) reported goals-outcomes linkages for midlevel employees. And only 17 percent reported such links for nonexempt employees.

Two other trends, one Orwellian, the other Darwinian, and both by-products of the simultaneous cooling of the talent wars and the economy, suggest a more exacting and tougher edge to performance management strategies. The first of these trends involves tighter, electronically aided performance measurement. According to an article in *Business Week*, an increasing number of companies are adopting Web-enabled performance measurement technologies that enable them "to analyze with cold, hard data just how effective their ranks are."[7] While the technology is now most commonly deployed in telephone and online-based customer service settings—where capturing work output is a digital by-product of monitoring transaction data—it is reaching as well into other layers of work and performance.

One potential upside of this technology is its ability to more directly couple performance with incentive rewards so that, in the words of the *Business Week* article, "everyone from customer service reps to marketing execs can be paid in the modern equivalent of a piece-rate system." But, of course, this upside contrasts with an ominous, Big Brother downside: the potential of intrusions into talent privacy so pervasive and overbearing that the workplace risks becoming a setting for conflict rather than engagement.

A second postboom performance management trend—the increasing popularity of forced-ranking processes—is raising the stakes of performance management outcomes. Forced-ranking in its purest form involves ranking everyone in a company, division, or department from best to worst, in an effort to determine how to allocate pay and/or implement workforce reductions. The systems—now commonly and caustically termed *rank and yank*—have spread to some 20 percent of U.S. companies, among them major employers such as Conoco, Ford Motor, Microsoft, Sun Microsystems, and (notoriously) Enron.[8] Employers who force-rank generally align employee evaluations with predetermined performance distribution percentages. Evaluators end up making determinations on a person-versus-person basis rather than a person-to-established-standards basis.

Sun Microsystems ranks its forty-three thousand employees in three groups: 20 percent are superior; 70 percent are Sun Standard; 10 percent are underperforming. (See Exhibit 7-1.) The company then alerts underperforming staff to their tenuous status and provides one-on-one coaching to help redeem their performance.[9]

GE has been one of the pioneers in this process. Jack Welch, in a letter to GE shareholders, similarly differentiated among the top 20 percent of employees, the bottom 10 percent, and the middle 70 percent:

> Not removing the bottom 10 percent early in their careers is not only a management failure, but false kindness as well—a form of cruelty—because inevitably a new leader will come into a business and take out that bottom 10 percent right away, leaving them—sometimes midway through a career—stranded and having to start over somewhere else.

Hewlett-Packard (HP), long a bellwether of talent strategy trends for the traditional employment model, is a recent convert to forced distribution performance management. CEO Carly Fiorina described HP's newly stringent evaluation process (where talent is evaluated on a 1-to-5 scale, with 15 percent getting 5s—the top rating—and 5 percent getting 1s) as "going back to performance management the way it was originally intended to be."[10]

What is the place of these survivor processes in a company's talent strategies? One point of reference is to consider data on strategic-versus-nonstrategic efforts by companies to prune their workforces. Economists Geoffrey Love and Nitin Nohria, in a study of downsizing at *Fortune* 100

Exhibit 7-1. Forced ranking performance management.

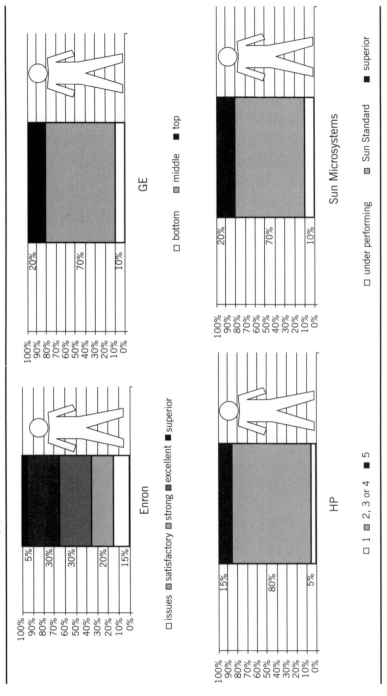

companies from 1977 to 1993, measured the links between company stock performance and job cuts, differentiating cuts prompted by strategic restructuring and those done in hasty response to short-term market fluctuations and falling profits. Their findings indicate that strategy-based cuts were associated with above average short- and long-term share performance, nonstrategic cuts, by contrast, with prolonged underperformance. If this linkage holds, the question remains: When do these processes make strategic sense? The answer, not surprisingly, is when they align with business strategies and culture: in particular, when they are backed by performance information that justifies the outcomes; and when they include many channels to soar as well as one to fail.

Judging the Enron process against this standard, it may indeed have been on strategy. Forced-ranking of performance was certainly "on culture," especially in the competitive, high-risk (and high-reward) environment of the wholesale-energy trading unit where the company piloted the process ten years before extending it to all its Houston-based talent. And while the process may have been draconian, its results were also based on explicit top management reviews using information from multiple sources. For example, Enron staff could turn in self-assessments and choose up to seven colleagues or clients to write evaluations on their behalf. Moreover, anyone in the company could voluntarily submit a review of someone else's performance.

For GE (where the experience with the methodology likely prompted its rising popularity among other employers) forced distribution is only one piece of a fully established talent assessment and development strategy in a company with an acknowledged reputation for continually raising the bar on performance.

Forced distribution performance management may also be a strategic fit for companies whose health or survival is based on time-pressured changes in workforce size or composition (HP, for example), especially if the alternative is slash-and-burn cuts without systematic consideration of talent contributions. But, as a first and primary talent strategy initiative for improving performance levels, forced distribution performance management initiatives make questionable sense. For one thing, their use is at least a tacit concession that recruiting processes bring in prospects whose performance is—or ends up—on the wrong side of the distribution curve; in this sense they point back to the need to improve talent flow quality. Dropped out of the blue, they stir suspicion and discourage information sharing, cooperation, and teamwork. They can also be dangerous to a company's legal health, especially where forced rankings are applied to talent in small groups, or where ranking results do not show clear distinctions yet adverse actions occur using those distinctions. The processes used at Microsoft, Ford Motor, and Conoco have all attracted lawsuits, with plaintiffs claiming systems illegally favor some groups of employees over others: white males over blacks and women, younger managers over older ones, and foreign citizens over U.S. citizens. Ford Motor, for one, has retreated from its program.

Successful performance management can get off to a better start with infrastructure basics: links between business strategies and quantifiable individual goals; communication initiatives that help individuals understand their contribution to the overall business; and processes that link behavioral objectives to personal development, unbiased feedback, and commensurate rewards.

It is this sort of infrastructure that forms the basis of a talent strategy initiative currently underway at specialty retailer Lands' End. Tom Gloudeman, the company's director of professional recruiting and development, partnering with Genesys Software Systems of Methuen, Massachusetts, is overseeing the building and deployment of a competency management system incorporating essential talent competencies at Lands' End. The system is designed to link competencies (at the company, division, team, role, and position levels, based on a structured model provided by Personnel Decisions International) to learning resources/opportunities and to individual development plans. The system—being rolled out in stages to Lands' End departments, initially to its information systems group—is seen as a step toward integrating competencies into recruiting and learning (of all types), so that talent development will follow more naturally and more in line with business strategy.

The resulting information base, among other things, equips managers with tools that can couple performance feedback (the past and present) with individually customized development plans (the future).

Learning

As we saw in Chapter 3, business-based training under the traditional employment model was both a benefit and a shackle. Learning was often extensive, but it was also company specific. Receiving it increased the employee's value to the organization and better secured his or her job. However, the training content did not improve the employee's chances for entry in other industries or even into competing companies—the training and the experience it led to had relatively little value to other employers.

Even the internal career payoff for learning was neither quick nor predictable. Much learning came from observing and practicing in an understudy role; trainees often waited long years for a step up the rung and a chance to actually apply what had been learned—with the expectation it was still relevant. It was this type of learning—apprenticelike, experience-driven, and job-specific—that has faded under more contingent employment arrangements. In effect, many employers moved away from growing talent internally, opting instead to buy talent skills on the open market as needed and to restructure their workforces as necessary to shed outmoded skills.

What is the place of business learning in today's customer-focused business strategies and contingent-employment talent strategies? First, from a resource perspective, the following are basic reported numbers for the industry:[11]

- In 2001, direct costs for training at U.S. companies typically amounted to 2 percent of payroll; at the high end of this scale are payroll allocations in finance, insurance, and real estate (2.8 percent); transportation and public utilities (2.7 percent); and technology (2.5 percent).
- Total training expenditures on a per employee basis averaged

$704; however, companies that reported making a dedicated com-
mitment to developing their employees spent an average of
$1,574.

- Learning content is weighted toward technical processes and procedures, IT, managerial/supervisory skills, occupational safety,
and product knowledge.

As is the case for recruiting resources, these hard dollar numbers
undoubtedly understate actual resource use. Indirect and opportunity
costs (lost productivity during periods of off-site training, for example)
may inflate the total to 10 percent or more. On top of this, the costs of
investments in informal training may well be at least as large as formal
program investments. It is this scale that makes business learning seem
like a resource risk to employers, especially in industries and work settings stripped of job security—from the employer's perspective, the removal of the employment continuity that made it possible to recoup
learning costs with learning-related productivity.

But, in the era of customer-focused strategies, companies are also
finding unacceptable risks in not making learning available, as well as
significant opportunities in reconfiguring and expanding its availability.
Via Web-based technologies, companies are discovering ways to deliver
training more easily and in smaller, more interactive, applicable, and
cost-effective bites. Finally, they are finding that learning is a value-
chain necessity. Although employed talent is a crucial link in the learning value-chain, it is only one link. Other links include customers, vendors, suppliers, distributors, contractors, venture partners, and even
talent prospects. Learning is something that companies increasingly find
counterproductive to hold close to the vest or to parcel out only to a
selected inner circle.

Most companies of any scale now use Web technologies for some
level of value chain information exchange—in some instances intranet-
based (that is, within enterprise boundaries); in others extranet-based
(outside enterprise boundaries to include vendors, suppliers, distributors, or other partners); in still others Internet-based (to post or deliver

information on prices, product specifications, ordering information, customization options, design criteria, order and delivery status, invoicing, and all sorts of other value-chain information). For early adopter companies such as Cisco, Ford Motors, Dell, HP, Nike, Nortel, Oracle, and United Parcel Service (UPS), this information exchange is merely the first stage of what has evolved into innovative, interdependent, and online-mediated extended enterprise arrangements. Under these arrangements, and based on company competencies, value chain partners take over entire segments of design, manufacturing, distribution, and other functions that used to be self-contained within each company's boundaries. For examples, because of proximity to product end users, UPS provides repair services and financial services as well as delivery services for high-technology customers. Goodyear handles tire warehousing and delivery logistics for Navistar truck manufacturing. Cisco virtually integrates its manufacturing, logistics, and distribution into a single enterprise program (SEP), which includes a number of contract partners.[12]

This extended enterprise trend has several important implications for talent learning strategies. First, the Web-based technologies that enable the extended enterprise also enable business e-learning: A phenomenon whose economy-wide scope, according to Cisco CEO John Chambers, will "be so big it is going to make e-mail usage look like a rounding error," and whose business-learning version now accounts for upwards of 8 percent of businesses' direct expenditures for learning.[13] Increasingly, value chain information either directly provides content or speeds the development of e-learning content. As just one example, 80 percent or more of Oracle product training material is released electronically on the same day as the product itself.[14]

Just as fundamentally, the extended enterprise is escalating the need, speed, and complexity of things that talent must master—and therefore the need, speed, and complexity of learning requirements. As companies such as Cisco and Nike concentrate on design and customer relations, its talent must master a dizzying volume of complex information and be fluent with it during customer- and partner-facing real-time interactions, both online and by telephone. For example, 40 to 60 percent of Cisco's annual revenue comes from products developed within the previous twelve months.[15]

This means that learning in companies such as Cisco goes through compressed cycles of immediacy and obsolescence. It also means that learning is constant and more than ever apt to be indistinguishable from work. In other words: "Learning is not something that requires time out from being engaged in productive activity; learning is the heart of productive activity. To put it simply, learning is the new form of labor."[16] E-learning arrangements enable this work/learning fusion for learning requirements that do not involve the need to convene.

Work/learning fusion in turn means that talent-learning initiatives need to deliver and manage more individualized learning plans combining classroom training with e-learning and with actual business experiences. Using this blended approach, vague concepts of "employee development" transform into individual engagement plans that tie specific learning needs to specific real-time business needs as, for example, at Lands' End.

When mass customized in this way, company-based learning has been shown to have payoffs in containing costs and promoting talent engagement. For example, according to the 2002 Hackett Best Practices survey of HR practice benchmarks, learning and development costs decrease by 60 percent when talent-learning initiatives are based on individual plans tied to company strategy. And, in using such plans, companies report being able to promote internal candidates 230 percent more often than do companies without such plans.

An example that showcases these learning strategy components is American Skandia, the Connecticut-based U.S. arm of the international savings and insurance company. When Rebecca Ray, currently senior vice president and director of training, joined American Skandia in November 1999, the company's employee formal learning programs consisted of a typical and limited mix of instructor-led courses in customer service, desktop applications, and sales. Ray realized immediately that

American Skandia's talent learning needs were complex, dynamic, and urgent.

American Skandia offers financial products through broker-dealer firms rather than directly to the public. This means that American Skandia salespeople must understand and be able to explain the features of an entire portfolio of products instead of a single specialized line, a real challenge when it comes to educating, certifying, and continually reskilling a decentralized sales and support workforce. Because the savings and insurance industries are heavily regulated, employees must have current credentials and must also be fluent with the latest regulations in their interactions with investment professionals. Finally, since American Skandia relies on a sizeable network of investment professionals who handle many other financial service products, these value chain "customers" also require extensive—and efficient—learning resources.

In response to these needs, Ray made a business case for creating a comprehensive corporate university with an e-learning core. With the support of American Skandia CEO Wade Dokken, partnering to meet the needs of key leadership stakeholders, and relying heavily on internal resources and sweat equity, Ray and her team were able to launch American Skandia University (ASU) on March 31, 2000, just five months from its original conception. In its current configuration, ASU offers blended learning options that include instructor-led classes, self-study, and online learning. The e-learning offerings are in turn divided into three formats, scaled for different levels of complexity:

- Desktop software applications and advanced IT professional topics
- Industry-specific training in topics such as annuities, financial regulations, and business ethics
- Company-specific topics such as antifraud policies and products and services

Every American Skandia employee has access to e-learning opportunities by logging onto the ASU Web site and completing modules at their own pace between assignments, before or after hours, on-site or at home. Distributing learning electronically also enables American Skandia wholesalers in different locations to learn when it is convenient for them while traveling on business. And the immediacy of Web-based information eases the burden of instantly updating learning materials to incorporate changes such as new product information or new government regulations.

ASU is an initiative that crosses traditional enterprise boundaries by extending learning to talent in partner companies. But learning can also cross boundaries to talent prospects, in the process supporting two talent flow objectives: first, as a value-added inducement to begin the sorts of preemployment relationships we described in Chapter 6; and second, to considerably enhance the talent flow to talent engagement transition we described earlier in this chapter.

Providing services in this talent strategy frontier is a company called PicturePeak, (www.picturepeak.com), a New York City–based start-up that has built what it terms a skill-based recruitment system aimed at "accelerating new-hire productivity." PicturePeak, which bills its services to client companies (currently including financial services clients such as Prudential and MBNA), targets talent making under $75,000. PicturePeak CEO David Hertz identifies this as a segment that makes up about 90 percent of the U.S. talent marketplace; and a segment that is typically underserved when it comes to career-based learning and development.

PicturePeak focuses its efforts on assisting talent prospects (members) and employers by closing the gaps between employer skill needs and member skills achievement. Instead of submitting resumes, members who enter and register at the PicturePeak site are guided through the preparation of a skills transcript, which documents skills attained through combinations of work and education. (The skill categories include managing resources, managing information, interpersonal skills, managing systems, managing technology, thinking skills, and basic skills.)

Employer job-posting requirements are similarly presented in terms of skills. Job matches occur when employer skill needs for employer-posted jobs coincide with member skills attainment; and employers can specify the minimum level of skills needed to qualify as a match.

To assist in closing skill gaps, members are pointed to resources such as assessment tools and e-learning course materials. Low-cost course materials in each of the skill categories may be provided through third-party e-learning vendors. However, materials may also come directly from employers. Learning through these sorts of employer-specific materials can lay the groundwork for initial preemployment relationships; it can also fast-track the talent flow/talent engagement transition.

Rewards

In many ways, rewards define the talent-employer relationship. Rewards are the most tangible expression of the relationship. Rewards are what you get in return for what you give in performance and commitment. While financial rewards may not provide the initiating motivation to perform, they provide the necessary means of exchange without which performance won't endure.

Rewards systems that are effectively designed and flexibly managed do more than distribute cash to employees. They reinforce the behaviors or the results—or both—that support business strategies. They can adapt to market realities and skillfully influence levels of employee commitment and discretionary effort—in other words, engagement.

Of course, the opposite is also true. Reward programs can be designed inflexibly or be run to unfairly exploit the employment relationship. They can also demonstrate that there is no accountability, that performance and reward outcomes are either unrelated (random) or inversely related (punishing).

Under ideal circumstances, flexible reward systems can position and deliver on a powerful strategy-based proposition: If people's actions support business's mission, values. and objectives, and these actions improve financial performance, then they can legitimately expect to be enriched in proportion to their contributions and commensurate with other opportunities that the marketplace might offer them. Clearly, the rewards process can influence outcomes in talent recruiting, performance management (engagement), and talent retention.

However, if flexibility and responsiveness to performance and market are key, then relatively few companies operate rewards processes in ways that support talent strategies. Evidence here comes from a survey of HR executives by the consulting firm Towers Perrin. Exhibit 7-2 shows that only a handful of those companies surveyed customized—or had the flexibility to customize their reward packages to meet the needs and match the performance of individuals. Although survey results suggest upcoming improvements, there is clearly a way to go.

For many companies the real concern about rewards is talent flow and cost economy: whether they're paying the correct amount (enough but not too much) to attract and retain the necessary revenue-driving talent. One by-product of the new employment market, the general erosion of long-term employment relationships, and the greater reliance on

Exhibit 7-2. Employer ability to customize reward packages.

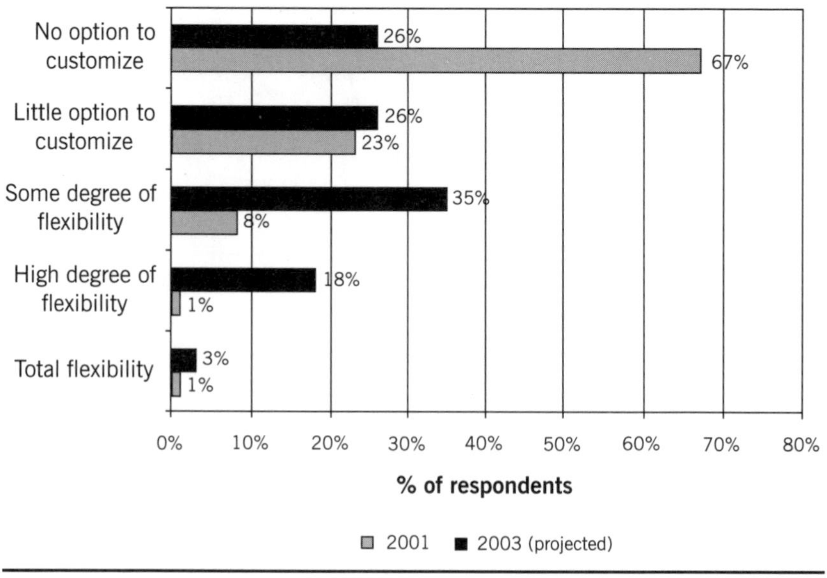

No option to customize: 26%, 67%
Little option to customize: 26%, 23%
Some degree of flexibility: 35%, 8%
High degree of flexibility: 18%, 1%
Total flexibility: 3%, 1%

% of respondents

☐ 2001   ■ 2003 (projected)

Based on data from Towers Perrin.

external recruiting to fill talent opportunities at all levels is a commensurate reliance on how the outside values talent. The so-called outside may include direct competitors for products and services or talent competitors—those who compete for the same talent by specific profession, by geography, or by other factors. For example, in a recent SHRM/Ohio State University survey of 571 companies, roughly two-thirds indicated that pay rates are determined primarily by market rates for similar jobs.[17]

On the engagement side, incentive rewards can be mobilized to focus immediate attention on strategy priorities such as product quality or customer focus or teamwork. Through equity, in the form of stock ownership for public companies, reward initiatives can provide employees a direct stake in business success and a line of site to how the business is valued by investor markets.

Rewards need not always be in cash form—other forms can sometimes provide greater leverage. Indeed, if the reward is cash, it generally takes 5 to 8 percent of an employee's salary to change behavior, according to data from the American Productivity & Quality Center in Houston and World at Work, the Scottsdale, Arizona–based organization for reward professionals. By contrast, the behavior-leveraging differentiation for noncash rewards is about 4 percent.

The most recent talent wars combined with the entrepreneurial psychologies of the growth economy and a free-agent nation to stir talent's appetite for risk, incentive, and equity. For example, in its 2000 U.S. Salary Increase Survey, Hewitt Associates reported that 78 percent of surveyed organizations had at least one type of variable pay plan in place for salaried exempt employees—an increase over the 1999 level of 70 percent. A 2001 study of New Jersey–based technology companies conducted by our firm corroborated this trend: 90 percent of companies participating in study had one or more variable reward plans in place. What changed during the employment boom were the frequency, variety, and sophistication of variable rewards. For many small employers, variable reward plans created leverage and competitive advantage in going head-to-head with large employers. For key talent they became the currency of new employment arrangements.

Equity participation programs also surged—for publicly-traded companies in the form of stock options, stock grants, and stock purchase programs; for privately held companies in the form of phantom stock or participation units. An August 2000 survey of nine hundred World at Work member companies found that 51 percent of surveyed companies offered a stock-based reward plan; most of these (94 percent) were in the form of stock options to leadership, professional, technical, sales, and administrative talent. Even as the market cooled in 2001, a repeat of the survey found the percentage of companies offering some sort of equity participation program had increased to 66 percent. Not surprisingly, this trend was even more evident in high-tech companies and companies that conducted initial public offerings (IPOs) in the late 1990s. A World at Work survey of eight hundred companies in these industry segments found that 84 percent offered stock-based compensation plans; and of these, 96 percent offered broad-based plans, making most or all company employees eligible for participation.

While variable pay arrangements are most often structured to be performance drivers, during the height of the talent wars they also became significant talent flow levers. Closing join-or-stay deals for key talent frequently hinged on signing bonuses, nonrecoverable draws on sales commissions, or other reward arrangements that were often variable in name only, and were neither contingent nor at-risk. March 2000 data from World at Work member company survey data showed 60 percent of companies using sign-on bonuses, and 88 percent of those using them believing they benefited recruiting efforts, while 30 percent reported having some form of retention bonus program in place.

Obviously, as the talent wars cooled down so did the penchant for talent acquisition bonuses. However, at the same time, retention-based reward programs seemed either to stay in place or grow, perhaps recognition of the steep investments made in key talent. A March 2001 repeat of World at Work's 2000 retention bonus survey (using the same group of respondents) showed a 10 percent increase in the number of companies having such programs. Retention bonus use increased significantly for leadership talent (up 28 percent) with other significant use targeted to middle management, professional, and IT talent (see Exhibit 7-3).

The trick for salary-, variable-, and equity-based rewards is separating initiatives that make business sense from ones that do not. Reward programs become headaches mostly to the extent that they are used needlessly, inequitably, or unaccountably. They become effective tools when their use aligns with business strategies. The distinctions can sometimes lead to surprising results that, at first glance, may seem to contradict industry expectations. But, ultimately, that is part of the point: talent strategies that differentiate the employer while supporting its business strategies. The key to the reward initiatives we describe next is often that, when it comes to pay, they position the talent value proposition on a new and different competitive plane.

Consider SAS, for example, the software technology company where the investment in benefits and work/life amenities seems to have had an impact on talent flow. As a privately-held company, SAS does not offer its employees stock options or similar highly leveraged equity

Exhibit 7-3. Use of retention-based rewards.

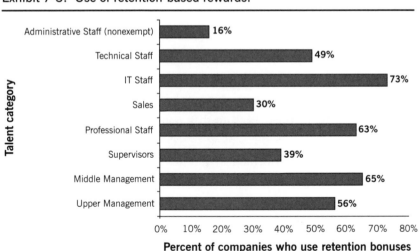

Based on data from the 2nd annual Retention Bonus Survey conducted by WorldatWork; 550 total rewards professionals; March 2001.

opportunities in an industry where such arrangements seem de rigueur (witness the World at Work survey results for high-tech and IPO companies). It turns out that logic is on SAS's side—and very much in line with its business and talent strategies. For many people during the employment boom, stock options had become like the lottery: Get a ticket, hope to strike it rich, and then quit. In other words, it may not always make strategic sense—and for SAS it doesn't in the overall context of their talent strategies—to install a pay component that motivates their best talent to come to work so they can make enough money to leave.

Conversely, the nonprofit sector would seem to be the last place to look for performance leveraging incentive rewards. Yet, for East Alabama Medical Center, a pioneering organization-wide gain-sharing program has been the signature feature of its reward programs. The program, now entering its sixth year of operation, generates payments to EAMC employees according to formulas that incorporate results from semiannual patient satisfaction surveys and annual bottom-line financial results. (Plan payments are made twice annually based on patient satisfaction survey results, once annually based on financial results.) Executive management sets the gain-sharing pool; a gain-sharing planning team then determines distribution criteria.

The gain-sharing program's origins trace to a strategic determination by hospital leadership about the value proposition that EAMC should convey to its talent community. Instead of bidding for talent by incrementally upping the base pay ante in each competitive recruiting situation, EAMC stepped back to differentiate its reward program as long term and demonstrably linked to balanced and consistently progressing organization performance. In other words, it would be a reward feature attractive to career-minded talent with payouts that would reward team efforts.

Two other features further distinguish the program. The first is its attainability. Terry Andrus, EAMC's president, determined that a crucial aspect of launching and succeeding with the program would be that it actually delivers payments. Initial program goals were set with this in mind and attainability continues to be a planning consideration. The underlying idea was to create and renew success by demonstrating success.

The second feature is communication. Each of EAMC's hiring managers has access to a total rewards estimator, a software tool that can produce printed or online estimates of gain-sharing value for talent prospects and employees in the context of EAMC's overall rewards package. This has proved to be a powerful recruiting and retention tool says Susan Johnston, EAMC's director for human resources; it gives managers a tangible, real-time, and objective way of conveying EAMC's talent value proposition. No other regional employer, public or private, has a feature that can directly compete with it. Further, total rewards estimator results appeal most to the kinds of talent that EAMC most wants to acquire.

If the nonprofit sector seems to be the last place to look for incentive-based pay, then specialty retail might similarly be the last place to look for pacesetting base pay. But, at The Container Store, whose (low) retail industry pacesetting turnover we mentioned in Chapter 6, and whose (high) industry pacesetting investment in learning we just cited, salaries also outpace industry norms: Salespeople at The Container Store generally start with annual salaries of around $45,000, with 8 percent raises a year for excellent sellers. To store leadership, retail pay leadership is a complementary component of its talent flow and engagement strategies: selective hiring to fit store values; extensive training to boost sales; and retention enabling pay to protect its talent selection and learning investments.

After the current pause in the talent wars, it will be increasingly important to broaden the concept of total pay to encompass new and flexible arrangements. We think it is likely that such arrangements will increase in importance, giving savvy employers and knowledgeable talent ways of striking mutually advantageous employment deals. For companies the key is to better manage, mobilize, and value these arrangements. By looking "far off" at today and "close up" at a different future, we suggest a new path—taking what now may seem to be creative compensation headaches to a new more flexible, more fully integrated and competitive level.

Notes

1. Robert Galford, "Why Doesn't This HR Department Get Any Respect?" *Harvard Business Review*, March–April 1998, pp. 24–39.

2. Bill Birchard, "Hire Great People Fast," *Fast Company*, August 1997, p. 132.

3. Gina Imperato, "How to Give Good Feedback," *Fast Company*, September 1998, p. 144.

4. Michelle Conlin, "The Software Says You're Just Average," *BW Online*, February 25, 2002.

5. Imperato, p. 144.

6. Results are based on responses from 480 HR professionals, all of them SHRM members.

7. Conlin.

8. The Enron process, which ultimately covered 60 percent of Enron staff, put employees in one of five categories: 5 percent to be identified as superior, 30 percent as excellent, 30 percent as strong, 20 percent as satisfactory, and 15 percent as needs improvement or has issues. With rankings based on relative performance, it was possible for someone to perform at the same or higher level than before yet receive a lower rating if other employees' performance raised the bar. Source: L.M. Sixel, "Enron Rating Setup Irks Many Workers," Houston-Chronicle.com, February 5, 2001.

9. John Greenwald, "Rank and Fire," *Time*, June 11, 2001.

10. Michelle Quinn, "Performance Reviews Return with a Vengeance," *San Jose Mercury News*, August 8, 2001.

11. American Society for Training & Development, *2002 State of the Industry Report*. The report includes findings from 367 U.S. organizations that participated in ASTD's Benchmarking Service during 2001 and provided sufficient amounts of valid data on their training activities during 2000 and the latter part of 2001.

12. Michael Hammer, *Agenda* (New York: Crown Business, 2001), p. 216.

13. Some companies already exceed this level: Management consulting firm Accenture, for example, expects that up to 70 percent of all of its business learning course offerings will involve e-learning delivery. Motorola projects that by 2003, 50 percent or more of its learning activities will be accomplished through e-learning strategies.

14. Anna Muoio, "Cisco Quick Study," *Fast Company,* October 2000.

15. Hammer, p. 212.

16. Shoshana Zuboff, *In the Age of the Smart Machine: The Future of Work and Power* (New York: Basic Books, 1988), p. 395.

17. SHRM/Fisher College of Business at The Ohio State University 2000/ 2001 "Human Resource Strategies, Stages of Development, and Organization Size" survey.

CHAPTER 8

☑ MEASURING AND IMPROVING TALENT STRATEGIES

STRATEGY MEASUREMENT IS DIFFICULT BUT strategy measurement matters. Grace Hopper, U.S. Navy admiral, computer pioneer, and one of the originators of the COBOL programming language put it this way: "One accurate measurement is worth a thousand opinions."[1] Nevertheless, strategies often stall around measurement issues. When it comes to performance measures, managers who think they agree on strategy suddenly find that they do not. But without commitment to measurement, it is both easy and deceptive to believe that everybody is on the same page, that everybody knows what is important, and that everybody knows how strategy initiatives are progressing. It rarely works that way.

Measuring value creation

How do people create value? How can you measure this value creation process and its impact on business results? These are essential questions for implementing talent strategy initiatives. While these are questions that highly admired companies seem to pursue, it is also true that these are questions that are left unanswered. One survey of senior HR managers found that formal measurements for vital issues such as turnover costs, talent economic value, training value, and work performance are seldom made by more than 10 percent of companies.[2] Reliable measures linking people to business strategy can impact decision-making and investment decisions. As it is, under financial pressure businesses frequently invest in physical capital at the expense of human capital because they are unconvinced of the value of people investments.[3]

Measurement perspectives: types, stages, and balanced measures

Measuring the success of business strategies and performance can be looked at from many perspectives. We narrow it down here to three: measurement types, measurement stages, and balanced measures.

Types: financial and process

Financial measures always describe monetary outcomes. Business financial measures can be separated further into those governed by financial accounting conventions and those based on general economic criteria. By contrast, process measures are more varied: Process measures can describe specific outcomes (what happened), but they also can evaluate the effectiveness, speed, or quality of work in progress (how effectively are things happening). Process measures can be taken in cost or revenue terms, but they can also involve other quantitative units—such as time, percentages, or numerical evaluations—or even qualitative criteria.

Talent strategy measures are most often process measures—reduced turnover, improved talent quality, and enhanced customer interaction behaviors—that, cumulatively, produce or contribute to minimizing costs and maximizing revenue. Unfortunately, this emphasis on process tends to obscure the impact and credibility of talent-based strategies. Financial objectives and results usually control the agenda for strategy making, organization structure, promotions, and rewards. Financial accounting results are geared for top management, enabling them to pull up the information needed to make decisions that then flow down.

A business organization without financial measures such as earnings growth, cash flow, return on equity, and return on sales is unlikely to be a viable business for long. However, the focus of these measures on past results (what was) versus ongoing process (how things are working as indicators of how they might improve) may create blind spots, particularly in customer-focused strategies. Financial accounting conventions are slow to adapt to the diversity of products, markets, and global competition or to support needed investments in technology.

As early as 1951, GE business strategists looked for alternatives to purely financial measures in measuring business results. The suite of measures they assembled, in addition to financial measures such as profitability, included process measures such as market share, productivity, employee attitudes, community responsibility, and a balance between short- and long-term goals. Ultimately, the measures made only modest inroads: the markets and the financial community demanded financial yardsticks and were indifferent to other measures.[4]

Beginning in the 1980s, however, widespread interest in total quality management (TQM), process reengineering, and customer relationship management (CRM) created an entirely new vocabulary of process measures: operational concepts such as error rate, cycle time, six sigma, benchmarking, and continuous improvement seemed to connect more easily and meaningfully with process effectiveness and the speed and quality outcomes that most mattered to customers. They are measures designed primarily for process participants—giving them near-term feedback for process evaluation and improvement. The logic of using these kinds of measures is that taking care of process cycle times or error rates or customer complaints ultimately leads to improved financial results.

But, just as past financial results are no guarantee of future financial success, huge strides in process excellence do not always pay off in the marketplace. The logic of this became painfully clear with the floundering of the Internet economy—where fanatic attention to market share, infrastructure, and customer relationships had often crowded out basic financial performance criteria. Even the undoing of Enron makes an argument for the importance of stricter and more traditional financial measures—and pulling back from some of the more entrepreneurial approaches to financial accounting.

Stages: strategic and operational

Another way to look at measures is through the perspective of time and strategic focus. Operational measures (financial and process) are metrics for short-term, ongoing annual cycle types of activities. Talent-based operation measures most often target short-term efficiencies and cost reduction. By contrast, strategic measures link to strategy objectives and strategy initiatives—they are measures of fundamental, sometimes dramatic change. We believe strategic measures are crucial to building the business case for talent strategy initiatives: payoffs for such initiatives are rarely immediate; at the same time, initial investments can have a substantial long-term upside—on both the cost and revenue sides of the business ledger.

Balanced measures

Faced with numerous measurement options, business leaders need to be purposeful, systematic, and selective in building a measurement repertoire. For example, if a company's strategy blends elements of customer satisfaction with logistics process excellence and short-term financial success, its strategy measures should likewise reflect an appropriate balance. This is the logic underlying the balanced scorecard, a methodology developed by Harvard Business school professors Robert

Kaplan and David Norton. Kaplan and Norton's approach advocates four perspectives:

1. Customer
2. Internal business
3. Innovation and learning
4. Financial

Incorporating these multiple perspectives into a set of measures, say Kaplan and Norton, ensures that both financial and process measures are considered; that different value criteria of outside and inside players are taken into account; and that offsetting improvements and setbacks (short-term financial results, for example, coming at the expense of operational quality and customer relationships) are equally visible.[5]

The balanced scorecard is one specific methodology for establishing a balance. Other important balancing considerations include the following:

• *Balancing critical and controllable.* Not surprisingly, what is critical is often not controllable, what is controllable is often not critical.[6] Market share, for example, is obviously a critical business strategy outcome. But it would be a stretch to directly connect any one business or talent process initiative to an outcome like this: Too many external factors play a part. Conversely, getting measures of everyday operations is often easy. Since what gets measured is what gets done, it is tempting to think that the more you measure, the more will get done. That is just not the way things work. It is important to discard measures—often the easiest ones—that do not support a strategic agenda. For example, process measures for talent acquisition abound, but such measures are not always relevant to business results or do not resonate with customers.[7] It is crucial to have strategies determine crucial measures rather than having strategies be governed by controllable measures that just happen to be in place.

• *Balancing "physician" and "coroner" measures.* Financial measures—profitability, return on investment (ROI), and discounted cash flow—are autopsy results. Although historical measures are useful, their value diminishes if they cannot be produced and communicated in time to make a difference. The fundamental language of business is about both work achievement and money. While businesses need a strong balance sheet and a good P&L, those are nevertheless outcomes. Managers often rely exclusively on these lagging indicators while ignoring fundamental but harder-to-measure process factors.[8] Effective measurement should include a blend of both.

• *Balancing value creation and cost reduction.* Many financial and process measures (return on investment, for example, and productivity) are expressed as efficiency ratios, often with something such as net income on top (the numerator) and something such as investment expenditure or headcount below. In this type of ratio, there are two ways to improve results, such as obtaining a higher ROI. One way, and typically the more challenging way, is to increase revenue. A second and easier way (at least up to—or down to—a certain point) is to cut investment, head count, or other costs. The point is that business strategies ultimately are designed to create wealth, not to cut expenses. Denominator measures—measures that exclusively emphasize cost cutting (lowering cost-per-hire or reducing learning expenditures)—will eventually create diminishing returns for most types of strategies.[9]

• *Balancing the needs of measurement audiences.* "Whose measures are these?" is always a relevant question to ask. Do not assume that measures for internal use will have meaning for external audiences. And do not assume that all audiences are the same. Talent strategies, like business strategies, have multiple customer audiences, including company leadership, hiring managers, talent prospects, current employees, and talent alumni.

Talent process measures

In this section and the next, we consider several of the most prevalent operational process measures for talent flow and engagement. In the chapter's final section, we will consider how these operation measures might be used to build a business case for talent strategy initiatives.

We've found that talent strategy outcomes indeed can have significant financial impacts. Certainly, if 80 percent or more of a company's expenditures are talent-related, then purposeful strategy initiatives are important levers for managing company costs (the denominator) and driving company revenue (the numerator). But this impact is often hard to gauge because of haphazard, incomplete, or nonexistent measures. Companies often settle for what they have without an effort to step back and rethink the measurement game, even when it is evident that the talent market is shifting.

It is useful to consider the steps you might take with a clean measurement slate (and many companies have such slates)—as a way of auditing the value of current measures (which ones might not be effective or are redundant and need to be rethought) and identifying missing measures (which should be adopted). A clean slate approach to developing talent process measures could use the following four-step approach:

1. Define the factors (for example, time, cost, quality, etc.) most important to process customers (for example, talent prospects or hiring managers).
2. Describe (map) the process (for example, recruiting, learning, rewarding) used to deliver results.
3. Identify the critical steps and competencies required for process success.
4. Design measures (for example, time, cost, service quality, process results) to track these steps and competencies.

Talent flow measures: recruiting

How much does it actually cost to hire someone? How much value does hiring bring? It depends on whom, how, when, and what you ask. Depending on your frame of reference, costs and value fluctuate widely.

Part of the problem is the quality and availability of the measures: what gets considered or counted or added up, and what does not.

The most frequently used recruiting process measure is undoubtedly cost-per-hire (CPH). CPH was first routinely calculated in the late 1960s by defense companies such as Raytheon and RCA to be included in contract proposals calling for the hiring of many similarly paid technical professionals in a single geographic area. CPH is calculated as:

Cost-per-Hire = (Total Recruiting Costs)/(Total Number of Hires)

The relationship is straightforward and works well under the circumstances for which it was originally devised—that is, many similar jobs within a limited geography. But, as typically used today, CPH leaves open a number of questions, among them just what do total recruiting costs consist of? In practice, total recruiting costs are often limited to hard-dollar costs—those easiest to capture—and exclude often-substantial infrastructure and internal staff costs. Limiting costs in this way keeps CPH artificially low. Using CPH also tends to blur the wide deviations in recruiting costs that occur even in small business organizations. At one extreme, if CPH data are combined into one measure that reflects all hiring from entry to executive level, the resulting average CPH may be accurate but not instructive. At the other extreme, CPH is apt to be captured for only a subset of hires, usually at the low end.

As calculated, CPH embodies the notion that the cheapest hire is always the best hire. It suggests a purely transactional process as opposed to a strategic process. It is a recruiter's measure used primarily by recruiters. This in turn raises the important issue of CPH's customer value. Indeed, a UCLA-affiliated study of the kind of information most valued by hiring managers conducted during the 1980s revealed an inverse relationship between what information was important to hiring managers and what information was important to recruiters. In essence, CPH information was of minimal interest to hiring managers.

In recent years, a new set of balanced recruiting measures has evolved through the research and data collection efforts of Staffing.org, a nonprofit consortium. In collaboration with the Society for Human Resources Management (SHRM), Staffing.org has also conducted (thus far) two annual surveys to collect nationwide data based on these new metrics. In the latest configuration, Staffing.org advocates the use of four balanced process measures, including a recruiting efficiency measure designed to replace CPH:

1. *New hire quality.* A rating (0 to 5 scale) by the hiring manager three to six months after hire, based on expectations prior to recruiting compared to actual performance.
2. *Time.* A time metric that compares the actual start date to the target start date jointly determined by recruiter and hiring manger.
3. *Hiring manager satisfaction.* A rating of satisfaction (0 to 5 scale) with the hiring process based on preestablished guidelines completed before and after the recruitment process.
4. *Efficiency.* Advanced as a more standardized recruiting process measure than CPH. The calculation for general recruiting efficiency (see Exhibit 8-1 for details) includes two new features: First, to account for variations that can occur as recruiting measures are applied to widely varying talent categories and salaries, this measure incorporates total compensation recruited as a leveling/index factor. Second, the measure is considerably more specific in defining the cost elements included in total staffing costs. Exhibit 8-2 displays a sample recruiting efficiency calculation.

In its 2000 survey, Staffing.org collected data from 679 organizations in thirteen separate business sectors covering over nine hundred thousand hires using both the CPH and recruiting efficiency measures. Selected findings are summarized in Exhibit 8-3, which compares selected CPH data ($) and recruiting efficiency data (percentage), highs and lows by industry, region, and employer size.

The data suggest that CPH and recruiting efficiency track in tan-

Exhibit 8-1. Staffing.org recruiting efficiency measure.

General Recruiting Efficiency = CostTotal/TCR

CostTotal = CostI + CostE + CostS + CostT

CostI (Internal Recruiting Costs): Expenses incurred regardless of actual recruiting; "operating expenses" or "internal or contracted expenses." Examples of costs included: salaries, office space, supplies, etc.

CostE (External Recruiting Costs): All external expenses incurred to identify talent candidates. Examples of costs included: advertising, contingency and retainer fees, research costs, annual fees for posting jobs on the Internet.

CostS (Signing Bonuses Costs)

CostT (Travel Relocation and Visa Expenses)

TCR (Total External Compensation Recruited): Sum of the base starting salaries for each external hire during their first year. *Note:* Part-timers working on an hourly basis should be included in this number; multiply their starting hourly wage by the hours they were expected to work over the first year.

---

dem, especially with CPH low and recruiting efficiency high. The consulting industry stands out with substantial recruiting expenditures (measured both in CPH and recruiting efficiency terms). This may reflect added care and rigor in selection of talent who are billable resources. Recruiting expenditures also tend to be higher for smaller employers (500 to 999 employees) than larger employers (5,000 employees and greater). The reason here is likely to be different: economy of scale. In other words, although small companies incur many of the same recruiting costs as larger companies, they are less able than larger companies to spread those costs across multiple hires.

Talent flow measures: retention/turnover measures

In Chapter 6 we described how one employer, SAS, uses an impressive array of employee benefits and work/life amenities both to leverage productivity and control employee defections. A multimillion-dollar

Exhibit 8-2. Sample recruiting efficiency calculation.

Assume the following annual recruiting and staffing data for a packaged consumer goods company:

- 952 positions filled
- $212,500 expended on search projects
- $1,350,000 spent on advertising
- About $625,000 spent on internal costs
- Average annual cash compensation for employees hired $53,500
- $560,000 for signing bonuses
- About $2,700,000 expended for relocation and visas.

$CostI = \$625,000$

$CostE = \$212,500 + \$1,350,000 = \$1,562,500$

$CostS = \$560,000$

$CostT = \$2,700,000$

$CostTotal = CostI + CostE + CostS + CostT$

$CostTotal = \$625,000 + \$1,562,500 + \$560,000 + \$2,700,000 = \$5,447,500$

Total Compensation Recruited $= 952 \times \$53,500 = \$50,932,000$

$$\text{Staffing Cost Ratio} = \frac{CostTotal}{TCR}$$

$$\text{Staffing Cost Ratio} = \frac{\$5,447,500}{\$50,932,000} = .107 = 10.7\%$$

projection of retention-based savings more than covers the tab. The projection in this instance assumed that replacement costs for a defecting SAS employee would be in the range of 1.5 times annual salary. The resulting calculation makes other assumptions as well:

- About the cost reduction and revenue increase potential of reduced turnover[10]
- About exactly how much turnover there would otherwise be
- About how directly talent strategy initiatives contribute to reducing turnover

Exhibit 8-3. 2000 Employment data comparing CPH and recruiting efficiency ratio measures.

Category	Cost-per-Hire ($) (low–best)	Cost-per-Hire ($) (high–worst)	Recruiting Efficiency Ratio (%) (low–best)	Recruiting Efficiency Ratio (%) (high–worst)
Industry	$2,181 Educational Services	$11,209 Consulting	6.3% Transportation	23.9% Consulting
U.S. Region	$2,492 Southeast	$8,126 Southwest*	11.7% Mid-North**	23.1% Southwest
Size (Number of Employees)	$3,519 5,000 and greater	$8,210 500–999	12.2% 5,000 and greater	18.7% 500–999

*Arizona, California, Colorado, Guam, Hawaii, Nevada, New Mexico, Northern Mariana, Utah
**Ilinois, Indiana, Iowa, Michigan, Minnesota, North Dakota, Ohio, South Dakota, West Virginia, Wisconsin

For a company deciding whether to undertake talent strategy initiatives in the interest of controlling turnover, making critical assumptions is unavoidable. The keys are being aware of the range of possible assumptions and then being realistic—that is, conservative—about the assumption(s) to use. Chapter 6 presented some data on annual turnover percentages. Exhibit 8-4 lists a sample of measurement yardsticks for turnover costs: The low figure from this collection of estimates is one-

Exhibit 8-4. Turnover costs.

Turnover rates

- The cost of replacing a worker runs between **1 and 2.5 times the salary** of the open job.
    SOURCES: *Hewitt Associates and the Saratoga Institute.*

- Conservative estimates place the cost of turnover at **25% of annual salary plus benefits.**
    SOURCE: *Kepner-Tregoe, Inc.*

- It costs a company **one-third of a new hire's annual salary** to replace an employee
    SOURCE: *U.S. Department of Labor.*

- A conservative estimate of employee turnover costs for a typical **healthcare system** ranges from **$14 million to $27 million per year.**
    SOURCE: *Total Compensation in Integrated Healthcare Systems: 2001 survey, Unifi Network, a subsidiary of PricewaterhouseCoopers LLP.*

- One out of every four nonacademic employees at Stanford University will leave the staff within the next year, if current turnover trends continue, the university says. Turnover costs Stanford about **$68 million a year,** according to a 1999 campus survey.
    SOURCE: *Silicon Valley/San Jose Business Journal, February 5, 2001.*

- Turnover directly costs the **IT industry $44 billion** on an annual basis. Based on 5.2 million front-line employees—systems analysts, programmers, and computer engineers; estimated turnover cost **55 percent of average salary** ($34,100 per employee).
    SOURCE: *Sibson & Co., as reported in ITworld.com.*

third of annual salary (from the Department of Labor), the high figure is 2.5 times annual salary (from consulting company studies).

Exhibit 8-5 extends this analysis further by presenting results obtained from using six online turnover calculators. The resulting range (expressed as a percent of annual salary, and as a dollar value using an $80,000 salary) is again considerable: from 9 percent to 202 percent.

Talent engagement measures: learning

Learning results are frequently measured using a four-level model developed by former ASTD president Donald Kirkpatrick. The model defines progressively more difficult and meaningful measures of learning effectiveness. Under the model, measures should begin at Level 1, and then, as time, budget, and expertise allow, move sequentially up through Levels 2, 3, and 4. Information from each lower level forms the base for the next higher level; in this way each successive level represents more precise, rigorous, and resource-intensive effectiveness measures. Brief definitions of the levels are as follows:

- *Level 1—Reactions.* This baseline measures a participant's initial reactions to business-learning experiences. While positive reactions do not guarantee learning, negative reactions suggest that learning has been minimal.

- *Level 2—Learning.* Evaluations at this level often involve content-based tests administered before (pretest) and after (posttest) training to assess how learning has advanced in terms of skills, knowledge, or attitude.

- *Level 3—Transfer.* Measures the transfer that has occurred in the learner's behavior due to training. Are the newly acquired skills, knowledge, or attitude being used by talent?

- *Level 4—Results.* Measures in terms of business process results: increased production, improved quality, decreased costs, reduced frequency of accidents, or increased sales.

Exhibit 8-5. Turnover calculator examples.

Calculator source	Calculated turnover cost[a]	% of base salary ($80,000)
1. Sibson cost of turnover calculator	$161,600[b]	202%
2. Turnover cost calculator, Integrated Management Resources, Inc.	$ 33,000[c]	41%
3. Cost of Early Employee Turnover, Advantage Hiring	$ 27,000[d]	34%
4. Staff turnover cost calculator, MXL, Australian-based employment services company	$ 19,567[e]	24%
5. Employee turnover cost calculator, SSS Consulting, Inc./The HR Chally Group	$ 16,716[f]	21%
6. Online employee turnover calculator, University of Wisconsin-Extension	$ 7,048[g]	9%

[a] Calculation based on one employee with annual salary of $80,000, using factors and factor values built into calculators

[b] Includes:
- Front Line employee costs associated with turnover: $60,800
- Supervisory and staff support costs associated with turnover: $33,600
- Opportunity costs (productivity costs of new employees; lost profit caused by reduced revenues due to turnover): $67,200

www.sibson.com/solution/retention/cot_calcuator/index_cotcalc.htm

[c] Based on "turnover cost percentage" of 33% of base salary plus benefits
www.imrtn.com/turnovercalc.asp

[d] Based on the model proposed by Saratoga Institute and Kepner-Tregoe Inc.
www.advantagehiring.com/calculators/ahi_calc_turnover.htm

[e] Includes:
- Cost of HR's Time: $240
- Advertising: $5,000
- Productivity Loss: $10,000
- Cost of Training: $962
- Cost of Coaching: $3,365

www.mxl.com/ia/TurnoverCalculator.html#OpportunityCosts

[f] Includes:
- Separation Costs: $2,288
- Replacement Costs: $941
- Training Costs: $13,487

www.chally.com/turnover_cost_calculator.htm
Downloads pdf document; requires Microsoft Excel, or an application that can open an Excel document

[g] Includes:
- Separation Costs: $3,088
- Vacancy Costs: −$7,000 (excess of saved salary and benefits over costs of temporary replacement)
- Replacement Costs: $5,950
- Training Costs: $5,010

www.uwex.edu/ces/cced/publicat/turn.html

From a business and organizational perspective, Level 4's results are the most desirable and meaningful. Yet, not unexpectedly, they also tend to be the measures that companies are least likely to capture; in the survey mentioned at the beginning of this chapter, for example, only about 6 percent of senior HR managers reported making formal estimates of the economic benefits of various training levels.

However, when Level 4 learning measures are captured, the results are persuasive that learning is an essential component of talent strategies. For example, in a 1997 ASTD-sponsored study, researchers looked at the training investments of 575 U.S.-based, publicly-traded firms from 1996 to 1998. Using a statistical model that controlled for characteristics such as industry, company size, prior financial performance, and earnings, researchers determined that an increase of $680 in a company's per employee training expenditures generated an average 6 percent improvement in total shareholder return (TSR) in the following year. When companies were ranked by learning expenditures, companies in the top half of the study group averaged a 36.9 percent TSR in the following year, which compared to a 19.8 percent average TSR for bottom-half companies. As a benchmark, the S&P 500 had an annual weighted return of 25.5 percent during the same period. In other words, TSRs for top-half companies were 86 percent higher than bottom-half companies, and 45 percent higher than the market-average TSR. Finally, comparing top-quarter learning expenditure companies to bottom-quarter companies, top-quarter companies enjoyed 24 percent higher financial profit margins and 26 percent higher price-to-book ratios.

Talent engagement measures: performance management

Results from the 2000 study of performance management processes cited in Chapter 7 give a hint of what is apt to be the norm for most organizations: Very seldom are performance management processes judged by their direct impact on company performance outcomes.[11] Instead, judgments center on process quality and acceptability. Data from Exhibit 8-6 reflect this reality. Only 12 percent of survey respondents (companies) evaluate performance management initiatives in terms of business goals; a greater percentage of companies—but still only 19 per-cent—evaluate performance in terms of individual performance goals. (See Exhibit 8-6.)

Strategic measures: cost-benefit analysis

Having considered a range of process measures, we turn here to how such measures might be used to build a case for strategy level talent initiatives. The process here typically involves comparing strategy initia-tive costs to initiative benefits; when conducting a cost-benefit analysis to evaluate strategic program initiatives, determining ROI is the under-lying strategic measure.

Calculating ROI involves some knowledge of finance, accounting, and capital budgeting. It also requires a conviction that talent in your company makes a substantial economic difference. The issue is not just that performance may be improved by investments in talent initiatives.

Exhibit 8-6. Measures of performance management effectiveness.

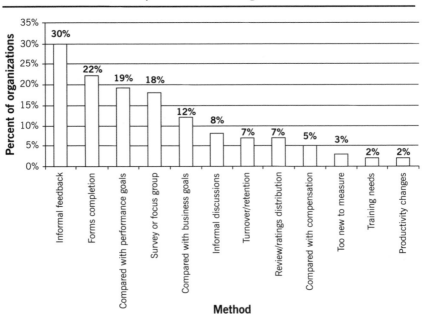

Instead, it is whether the performance improvement will happen soon enough and on a scale sufficient to justify the investment.

Calculating ROI requires assessing total costs and total benefits associated with a strategy initiative, and then calculating benefits less costs. The generic process is straightforward:

1. Identify potential costs
2. Identify potential benefits
3. Calculate the ROI using an appropriate index

Identifying cost and benefit categories and then attaching dollar values to them is part art, part science. Costs are generally easier to specify because they often represent tangible investments; they also occur earlier in the process. Benefits typically come later and are harder to define. More importantly, it is often difficult to ensure that benefits are tied to the strategy initiative and are not influenced disproportionately by other factors and events. The key is to come up with plausible estimates as well as a range of expected values for each estimate.

In calculating ROI for investments in talent strategy initiatives, we are interested in whether the initiative is worthwhile from an *economic* perspective as opposed to an *accounting* perspective.[12] Attaching accounting requirements to people-related investments does not always make economic sense. For example, for accounting purposes fixed costs such as buildings and equipment have multiyear value that is gradually depreciated over a period of three to five years. By contrast, investments in people—such as training or selection—are expensed during the year that they are incurred. If, using an accounting perspective, you do a multiyear analysis to determine the cost-effectiveness of people-oriented project investments, the people costs often pile up early and benefits do not show up until later years. Under accounting rules, such projects usually get off to a bad cost-effectiveness start—and have a lot of catching up to do.

ROI can be expressed in several ways. One way is to simply subtract costs from benefits. If benefits clearly exceed costs, then the investment is advisable. A second way to calculate ROI is to create a ratio or percentage from the same elements.

Determining ROI for strategy initiatives involves several additional complications. First, strategy level investments typically involve multi-year cost and benefit streams. For that reason, it is important to account for factors such as the time value of money: the reality that tomorrow's uncertain benefits (expressed in dollars) are not as valuable as today's certain dollars.

Net present value (NPV) is the factor used to take this time-value of money into consideration by appropriately reducing (discounting) future cash flows, usually in yearly increments and based on an assumed cost of capital. To see how this works, look at Exhibit 8-7 where the horizontal line represents a five-year period at the beginning of which an investment (the vertical line labeled *initial outlay*) is made in a

Exhibit 8-7. Net present value relationship.

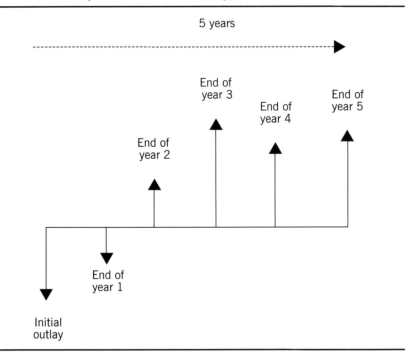

strategy initiative. At the end of each year the net benefits and costs resulting from the initiative are calculated (in dollar terms) and the result is shown as either negative (a downward pointing arrow as in year one) or positive (an upward pointing arrow as in years two through five).

NPV compares year-by-year benefits (combinations of revenue and cost savings) with cash outflow for investments in the initiative. The expected savings received each year and the ongoing cash outflows are both discounted by the cost of capital.[13] (For example, the dollar value of benefits in year five are discounted to enable an "apples to apples" comparison to the initial outlay dollars.) If net present value is greater than zero, the investment is acceptable. Looked at another way, when the present value of the benefits exceeds the present value of the investment outlays, the investment is acceptable as long as it occurs within the solution lifetime (for example, three to five years).

You can see already that cost-benefit analysis is less complicated for short-term investments. The challenge for most strategy initiatives, as we've said, is that benefits come later. On the other hand, the power of cost-benefit analysis is its ability to capture the longer-term payoffs inherent in well-designed strategy initiatives. We'll conclude by running simplified cost-benefit analyses for two talent strategy initiatives: one involving a talent relationship initiative, the other a learning initiative.

Cost-benefit analysis: talent relationship initiative

In Chapter 6 we discussed the value of talent relationship building in reducing the costs of talent acquisition and in improving talent quality. Talent relationship management involves adapting current talent acquisition practices and technologies to focus on proactively initiating, developing, and maintaining talent relationships (both preemployment and postemployment) in anticipation of future and long-term talent needs.

TRM strategy initiatives can involve a number of components: college recruiting, alumni communications, database building, digital marketing of opportunities, and other efforts. Multiple benefits might include better quality hires, reduced recruitment advertising, or reduced turnover. In this cost-benefit analysis example for a TRM initiative, we'll make the following assumptions related to an initiative to acquire, install, and use a TRM database.

- The initiative will be evaluated over a five-year period.
- Initial and ongoing investments in talent relationship database software and methodology: Software license $100,000 (prior to evaluation period); installation $60,000 (prior to evaluation period); ongoing software maintenance and technical support at $15,000 (15 percent) annually, beginning in the first year of the initiative.
- Annual reduction of external search costs, beginning with the second year of the initiative, reflecting the anticipation that key talent profiles will be in the database and that relationships with key talent will decrease the need for external search services. The projected reductions will be $90,000 in each of years two through four of the initiative and $120,000 in year five. Each external search is estimated to cost $30,000.
- A one-time increase in recruitment advertising of $200,000 (in the first year of the initiative) to assist in communicating and promoting the relationship initiative. Thereafter, there is an annual reduction of $100,000 in recruitment advertising expenditures, again reflecting an increased reliance on talent relationships.

The cost-benefit analysis results for this example are shown in Exhibit 8-8, which assumes an annual cost of capital of 12 percent. In this example, NPV for the five-year period of the initiative is positive ($101,943), indicating that, if assumptions hold true, the TRM strategy initiative will pay off in terms of cost savings alone.[14]

Cost-benefit analysis: learning initiative

Cost-benefit analyses can capture the impacts of increased revenue as well as decreased costs. While making these assumptions is more

Exhibit 8-8. TRM cost-benefit analysis.

	Initial initiative outlay	Discounted cash flow years 1–5	Cost-benefit results
TRM software license	− $100,000	$0	− $100,000
TRM software installation	− $60,000	$0	− $60,000
TRM software maintenance/ support	$0	− $54,072	− $54,072
External search costs	$0	$223,394	$223,394
Recruitment advertising	$0	$92,620	$92,620
NPV			$101,942
IRR			16.6%

risky, the possible payoffs can also be more substantial, and certainly worth considering. For example, we presented earlier the results of an ASTD-sponsored multicompany study that suggested the considerable impact on total shareholder return (TSR) for incremental additions to per employee learning expenditures.

This second cost-benefit analysis example looks within a company to evaluate the cost-benefit impact of a learning initiative targeted to increase talent's understanding of company business strategies. This cost-benefit analysis includes both projected revenue increases attributed to increased employee understanding; and reduced turnover costs (assuming that strategy understanding leads to increased talent engagement and commitment). The simplified assumptions are:

- The company has one thousand employees and the learning component of the initiative involves $500 in costs per person. The learning opportunity will be extended to all employees in the first year as well as to each new employee in subsequent years.
- The company has an annual turnover rate of 15 percent and the learning initiative is projected to decrease turnover by 20 percent (3 percentage points) to 12 percent annually, beginning with the

second year of the strategic learning initiative. Annual salaries average $50,000. Turnover costs for this example are limited to recruiting costs, based on a recruiting efficiency ratio of 15 percent.

- The company has current annual revenue of $20 million, projected to grow at 5 percent annually; the learning initiative is projected (conservatively) to increase each year's annual revenue by an additional 1 percent.

The cost-benefit analysis results for this example are shown in Exhibit 8-9, which again assumes an annual cost of capital of 12 percent.

Exhibit 8-9. Learning initiative cost-benefit analysis.

	Initial initiative outlay	Discounted cash flow years 1–5	Cost-benefit results
Learning costs	−$500,000	−$229,679	−$729,679
Savings from reduced turnover	$0	$610,182	$610,182
Increased revenue attributed to learning	$0	$609,439	$609,439
NPV			$489,942
IRR			42.3%

In this example NPV for the five-year period of the initiative is positive and substantial ($489,941). While different assumptions might increase or decrease NPV, the example suggests just how powerful a tool cost-benefit analysis can be in planning, justifying, and evaluating talent strategy initiatives.

Notes

1. Michael Hammer, *Agenda* (New York: Crown Business, 2001), p. 124.

2. Brian E. Becker, Mark A. Huselid, and David Ulrich, *The HR Scorecard: Linking People, Strategy, and Performance* (HBS Press, 2001), p. 94.

3. Ibid., p. 11.

4. Robert G. Eccles, "The Performance Measurement Manifesto," *Harvard Business Review on Measuring Corporate Performance* (Boston: Harvard Business School Press, 1998), pp. 28, 42.

5. Robert S. Kaplan and David P. Norton, *The Balanced Scorecard, Translating Strategy into Action* (Boston: Harvard Business School Press, 1996).

6. Hammer, p. 113.

7. One recent sample listed the six most common measuring points in the hiring process as: (1) Cost Per Hire (CPH); (2) Quality of Hire (QOH)—candidate qualifications compared with initial job requirements; (3) Time to Fill (TTF)—from position approval to candidate start; (4) Offer to Hire (OTH)—number of offers made to fill an opportunity; (5) Interview to Offer (ITO)—number of interviews conducted to fill an opportunity; (6) Route to Interest (RTI)—ratio of routed resumes to resumes of interest to hiring manager. Source: Kenneth Gaffey, "What Happens to Metrics During a Recession?" *Employment Management Today*, Winter 2002, pp. 11–15.

8. Daniel H. Pink, "Who Has the Next Big Idea?" *Fast Company*, September 2001, p. 108. (www.fastcompany.com/online/50/hammer.html).

9. Gary Hamel and C.K. Prahalad, *Competing for the Future* (Boston: Harvard Business School Press, 1994), p. 9.

10. The calculation details:

- A software company of SAS's size loses 1,000 employees per year.
- Because of lower turnover SAS loses about 130—which translates into almost 900 employees annually that SAS doesn't have to replace.
- SAS realizes savings that include lowered expenditures for recruiting and relocation.
- SAS also realizes revenues from employees who stay.
- Savings and revenue opportunities are calculated using a factor of 1.5 times annual salary and an average SAS annual salary of $50,000.
- $1.5 \times \$50,000 \times 900 = \$67,500,000$
- The results translate to $12,500 per year per employee that SAS can spend on benefits and work/life amenities.

11. The survey was conducted jointly by the Society for Human Resources Management and Personnel Decisions Incorporated, a Minneapolis-headquartered consulting company. Results are based on responses from 480 HR professionals, all of them SHRM members.

12. Becker, Huselid, and Ulrich, p. 85.

13. Given the risk characteristics of a talent strategy initiative, and the cost of funds under nonrisk conditions, an organization will select a discount rate, or cost of capital, at which to discount the flow of income from an initiative yield at present value. This risk-adjusted cost of capital can be based on bank rates, desired rate of return, potential external investments, and so forth.

14. Exhibit 8-8 also shows Internal Rate of Return (in this example approximately 17 percent). IRR is a financial calculation of rate of return on the cash flow, in total, over the life of the initiative. It equates the positive (incoming from cost savings in this example) cash flow with the negative (outgoing investment) cash flow associated with the project costs and is the rate at which funds are presumed to be reinvested.

◤ WHO OWNS TALENT STRATEGIES?

I N THEIR RESEARCH FOR *The War for Talent*, authors and McKinsey consultants Ed Michaels, Helen Handfield-Jones, and Beth Axelrod identify three distinct situations when client companies "get serious" about talent: The first is when there is a need to dramatically improve company performance and/or prospects for growth, coupled with the realization that upgrading the quality of key talent will be the prime driver. The second is when a company faces a hiring or retention crisis—as many companies did during the closing years of the last millennium. The third situation is a less crisis-driven but equally fundamental determination that, while current talent quality is good, talent management practices are not and will not enable the company to take the next step—

whether it is a growth initiative or a launch into a new industry.[1] The authors also concluded, after seeing little correlation between data on the quality of company HR talent processes and the level of company financial performance that it is primarily the mind-set of leaders throughout the organization that makes and sustains the success of talent initiatives.[2]

To this we add two perspectives. First, there are at least several studies that suggest a link between talent process excellence and financial results.[3] Second, strategic need and leadership mind-set are necessary but insufficient conditions for achieving strategic change. They will get the process going, remove initial obstacles and even kick it into high gear, but talent strategies, processes, initiatives, and execution will ultimately determine results. The question then is, Who conceives, plans, champions, and delivers talent strategies? In Chapter 4 we led with the assumption that it would be HR—although we left room for the possibility of other arrangements. Having presented our blueprint for full-cycle talent strategy planning, building, delivery, measuring, and improving, we conclude by assessing HR's fit for the demands and rigors of talent strategies.

The case for HR

Management guru Peter Drucker once pointedly quipped that an organization "puts together and calls 'personnel management' all those things that do not deal with the work of people and that are not management."[4] None of its activities either alone or combined, Drucker asserted, entitled personnel management to top management representation or justified the assignment of a top executive to the role. And, as a final blow, he observed: "[T]he personnel department as a rule stays away from the management of the enterprise's most important human resource, managers."[5] While Ducker first published these thoughts in his 1954 book *The Practice of Management*, it has survived in subsequent editions and, we think it's fair to say, in the minds of many corporate executives. Although it may be politically incorrect to claim that employees are anything other than "our most valuable asset," it's also fair to say that many opinions voiced about HR spare even empty praise.

In *The HR Scorecard: Linking People, Strategy, and Performance,* Brian Becker, Mark Huselid, and David Ulrich argue that while "executives want to believe that 'people are our most important asset' . . . they just can't understand how the HR function makes that vision a reality."[6] The result, they say, is that HR is often "on the table" rather than "at the table" when business strategy is decided and strategic roles are assigned.

Originally formed to take over tasks once performed by supervisors (most notably, recruiting) and to moderate some of the excesses of those same supervisors, HR began life as personnel administration—a collection of activities combining social services, record keeping, organizational housekeeping, and interpersonal firefighting. Its role has alternately broadened and contracted since then.

HR reached one high-water mark during the Organization Man era. Whyte described it as the "glamour one" among staff roles, its corporate population, according to one survey at the time, growing at a 15 percent annual rate. However, Whyte described its glamour image as "a mirage. The actual work is connected more with time study, aptitude testing, and stopwatches."[7]

Although HR long ago shed time study and stopwatches, it still maintains its reputation for handling embarrassing crises, disputes, severed employment, and other workplace disruptions involving people. To a certain extent, it has a vested interest in these headaches—and in being contacted when they occur. As much as HR professionals may be valued and appreciated when they respond to crises effectively, they also are criticized for not heading them off. More generally they get caught in a Pavlovian-style association: Managers are often unsure whether trouble leads to HR or vice versa.

Despite this mixed legacy, HR leaders are aspiring to strategic roles. Now, under the right conditions and with the right approach, many are actually succeeding—and many more could. Ironically, this success often has less to do with any roles or resources that have been added to HR's column, and more to do with what has been tightened or stripped away.

For example, the rounds of reengineering, outsourcing, cost cutting, and downsizing have cumulatively reduced HR's bulk and heightened its focus, in many cases transforming it from a specialized department to a cross-functional discipline with a much different distribution of process responsibilities—as displayed in Exhibit 9-1. What may have seemed—and what may still seem—like scorched earth management, has nevertheless redirected many HR minds to the strategic possibilities inherent in having to prioritize, innovate, and be resource conscious. In particular, the momentum toward the outsourcing of nonstrategic HR activities, depending on how you look at it, either elevates HR's strategy opportunities or backs HR into a corner.

As just one positive example of this phenomenon, when Dodge-ville, Wisconsin–based direct merchant Lands' End embarked in 2001 on preparation of its five-year strategic plan, Kelly Ritchie, Lands' End senior vice president of employee services, and Tom Gloudeman, direc-tor of recruiting and development, played lead roles in facilitating, coor-dinating, and communicating the planning process at all levels. The

Exhibit 9-1. HR's changing process responsibilities.

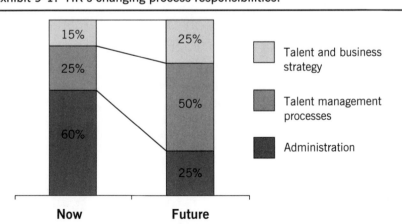

reasons? Lands' End HR had established its role as a valued process hub in a talent-centric business; further, it was equipped with the facilitation and communications expertise needed both to drive and build support for the process. And now, with the plan underway, HR has a continuing role, both as it meets its own strategic objectives and as it translates strategic objectives into strategy initiatives for key talent—one of which we profiled in Chapter 7.

Second, the strategy process in general has become more hands on. For large organizations, the planning and positioning approaches of the 1960s, 1970s, and 1980s were often elaborate exercises with planning staffs serving as ringmasters and gatekeepers. While today's customer strategies are hardly for amateurs, the organization of many large corporations in operationally autonomous strategic business units, the sprouting of thousands of smaller entrepreneurial companies, and the increasing compression of strategy life expectancy for all types of organizations generally mean that strategy participation is possible (although by no means guaranteed) for more organization players, HR not least among them. Indeed, in businesses that are stripped to the essentials there is not much room for key players who cannot contribute at the strategy level.

A third factor has been the increasing frequency and the increasing success of HR's efforts to decentralize into business partner structures. For large-scale corporate HR departments this has meant de-emphasizing or disbanding specialist function roles in favor of multidiscipline practice teams of HR business partners. HR business partners, assigned as individuals (or as teams with leads) to executives in key business areas, are supported by internal or outsourced practice centers to handle particularly complex issues or particularly high-volume transactions. As one HR executive, the vice president of global staffing for a *Fortune* 500 financial services company, said: "Tying into group-level and business unit objectives gives us the ability and flexibility to provide service as if we're in a smaller company setting."

This business partner psychology also extends to smaller HR staffs and to stand-alone roles in small organizations. While some HR holdovers may be business partners in name only, there is a real sense—certainly within the business organizations we've encountered—that the "way to play" is close to, rather than separate from, business strategies and objectives.

While all these transitional factors seem on balance to be pulling HR out of its administrative, reactive past and toward a more strategic future, it is still more destination than arrival. For example, by one estimate, fully 80 percent of HR organizations do not have a strategic plan that connects its resource allocations with enterprise strategy.[8] And by another estimate, HR organizations that lack that connection end up wasting upwards of 60 percent of their budget resources.[9]

At the other end of the spectrum, being lean and having to prioritize can be code words for being resource strapped and ineffectual. And, in the era of hands-on strategies, strategy formation removed from complexity-inducing planning staffs and planning processes can just as quickly pass to the jealous control of one or a handful of entrepreneurial leaders—resulting in a company comprised of one or several strategists and one hundred or one thousand assistants. Finally, a danger of the business partner model is that it can result in fragmented and disjointed approaches: HR can continue to operate reactively, only this time closer to the action.

Whether HR has a preeminent or secondary role, the fact remains that, for some very compelling reasons, being purposeful and focused about building effective talent strategies is crucial. As Chapters 1 and 3 made clear, talent represents a substantial organization resource, which has become such a pivotal strategy driver for customer-based strategies—and, owing to demographic trends, poses such a risk to organizations' ability to compete—that it clamors for strategic consideration. This can be achieved either as part of an integrated talent strategy plan whose champion and orchestrator is a strategically capable HR; or by expressly building talent strategy components into SBU or department strategies.

Regardless of the ownership arrangement, a deliberately strategic approach is the best way to handle and hold important ground when priorities and resource constraints are an unchanging way of life. Effective strategies make the best case for needed resources. In the talent arena, for example, priorities and resources that recently focused intensely on recruiting have now disappeared or shifted elsewhere. That does not make recruiting of key talent any less a long-term strategic issue. A talent strategies approach can be a way of keeping the pilot light burning on issues that may not be front burner now, but surely will be again. Integrated, effectively equipped, and continually communicated talent strategies are essential components in a customer-driven business economy.

Notes

1. Ed Michaels, Helen Handfield-Jones, and Beth Axelrod, *The War for Talent* (Boston: Harvard Business School Press, 2001), p. 160.

2. Ibid., p. 10.

3. In one study, researchers analyzed the financial performance of fifty-five publicly-traded companies on *Fortune* magazine's 1999 list of the "Best Companies to Work For," comparing the results to results from the Russell 3000 Index of U.S. stocks. Over the same five-year period, *Fortune*'s 55 "Best Companies" had an average annual appreciation of 25 percent when compared to a 19 percent average annual appreciation by the Russell index stocks.

In a second study, conducted jointly by consulting company Hewitt Associates, the University of Wisconsin, and Vanderbilt University, researchers analyzed the average stock returns from the 1993 "Best Companies" list for seven years and found that "Best Companies" results outpaced a broad market index of counterpart companies by 87 percent. In similar fashion, the 1998 *Fortune* companies bested their index counterparts by 56 percentage points, this time over four years.

Last, consulting company Watson Wyatt surveyed 405 publicly-traded companies to derive a Human Capital Index (HCI) based on factors such as workplace culture and communications. The surveyed companies were then sorted statistically into low, medium, and high HCI-rating categories and their financial results compared. High-HCI companies delivered a 103 percent total return to shareholders over a five-year period, compared with 53 percent for low-HCI and 88 percent for medium-HCI companies.

SOURCE: Tom Terez, "What Works: Build a Case for HR's Bottom-Line Impact," *Workforce,* March 2002, pp. 22–24.

4. Peter F. Drucker, *The Practice of Management* (New York: Harper & Row, 1982), p. 275.

5. Ibid., p. 276.

6. Brian E. Becker, Mark A. Huselid, and David Ulrich, *The HR Scorecard: Linking People, Strategy, and Performance* (Boston: Harvard Business School Press, 2001), p. 1.

7. William H. Whyte, *The Organization Man* (New York: Doubleday, 1956), p. 74.

8. Estimate from the Balanced Scorecard Collaborative.

9. From Hacket Best Practices 2002 benchmarking study of HR best practices.

◪ INDEX

Accenture, 179
administrative ineptitude, 144
administrative science, 63, 65
Akibia, 120, 123, 143
alumni relationships, 176–179
Amazon, 29
American Management Association, 80
American Productivity & Quality Center, 201
American Skandia Life Insurance Corporation, 121, 143–144, 196–198
American Skandia University (ASU), 197–198
America's Most Admired Companies, 118, 119
Amgen, 120, 121
Andrus, Terry, 204
annual cycles (business strategies), 51, 54
Annual Piece of Paper (APOP) program, 187
Aon Consulting, 186
APOP (Annual Piece of Paper) program, 187
Apple Computer, 69
applicant tracking systems (ATS), 150, 161
assets, tangible vs. intangible, 10, 11
assimilation consulting, 179
ASTD, 223
ASU, *see* American Skandia University
ATS, *see* applicant tracking systems
AT&T, 69
Axelrod, Beth, 233

baby boomers, 7, 80
Bain & Co., 123
balanced measures, 211–213
balanced scorecard, 211–212
Balanced Scorecard Collaborative, 143

Becker, Brian, 18, 235
Becker, Gary, 11
Being There, 182
belonging to, working for vs., 59–60, 82–83
best employers initiatives, *see* employer-of-choice initiatives
best-places-to-work lists, 120–122, 141n.4, 239n.3
Bloomberg, Michael R., 176
Bloomberg L.P., 176
BLS, *see* Bureau of Labor Statistics
boomerangs, 176
Boston Consulting Group, 38
bottom-up strategies, 51
branding, employment, 123–124
brand leadership, 10
Bristol-Myers Squibb Company, 119
budgeting, 51
building talent strategy, 118–140
    employer-of-choice initiatives for, 124–130
    employment branding in, 123–124
    objectives/initiatives in, 130–140
    talent value propositions in, 116–118, 120–123
Bureau of Labor Statistics (BLS), 8, 169
business-level competencies, 92–93, 155
business processes, 97–99
business strategy(-ies), 27–55
    barriers to understanding of, 28–31
    basic components for building, 115–116
    compatibility of organizational structure with, 93
    competency, 40–41, 47, 49–50
    contexts of, 33, 34
    customer-focused, 44–45
    customer value propositions in, 117–118, 121–122

business strategy(-ies) (*continued*)
  definitions of, 31–33
  efficiency, 41–43, 47, 50
  forms of, 45–50
  history of, 33–45
  integration, 35–36, 45–46, 48
  management cycles for, 50–57
  mission statements in, 116–117, 119
  models of, 33–45
  and other supporting processes, 30–31
  planning, 37–38, 46, 48–49
  position, 39–40, 46, 49
  shorthand, 43–44, 47, 50
  and talent history, 75–76
  and talent strategies, 90
  understanding of, 88, 90–91
  valuing talent during era of, 68
Business Week, 10, 50, 188

careers
  internal opportunities for advancement
    in, 66–67
  personal responsibility for, 72–73
Center for Effective Organizations (USC),
  168
Chambers, John, on business e-learning,
  195
Champy, James, 96, 97, 101
Charles Schwab & Co., Inc., 121, 123, 179
Chubb Group of Insurance Companies,
  178
Cisco Systems, 43
  alumni relationships at, 179
  business e-learning at, 195–197
  business-level competencies at, 92–93
  focus of, 48
  as one of 100 best companies to work
    for, 121
  talent engagement at, 184–185
clean slate approach, 214
Cleveland Cavaliers, 157
Colgate-Palmolive, 119
collective bargaining, 67
commitment
  employees' level of, 59–60
  free agency and, 73
  talent flow/engagement as replacement
    for, 80–83
communication
  of business strategies, 28
  performance management as, 187–188
  of talent flow strategies, 145–148
company culture, 115
company image, 168
competencies
  business-level, 92–93

downsizing for rearrangement of, 80–81
  recruiting use of, 154–159
  residing in employees, 71–72
  scanning of, 91–93
  strategy-level, 93
  talent flow strategy use of, 158–159
competency management system, 192–193
competency models, 155–157
competency strategies, 40–41, 47, 49–50
competitive advantage, 15, 70–71
computers, number of workers using, 77
Conference Board, 123
Conoco, 189, 192
consulting sector, recruiting costs in, 151
The Container Store, 78–79
  communication of strategy at, 147
  as one of 100 best companies to work
    for, 122
  retention at, 174
  rewards program at, 205
  talent engagement at, 185
  value propositions at, 143
Contemporary Strategy Analysis (Robert
  Grant), 33
contexts (of business strategies), 33, 34
contract workers, 82
controllable, balancing critical with, 212
core competencies, 49–50
cost-benefit analysis, 224–230
  of learning initiative, 228–230
  NPV calculation in, 226–227
  ROI calculation in, 224–226
  of talent relationship initiative, 227–228
cost-per-hire (CPH), 215–217, 219
cost reduction, value creation balanced
  with, 213
cost strategies, 40
CPH, *see* cost-per-hire
credibility, personal, 144
critical, balancing controllable with, 212
customer-focused markets, 71
customer-focused strategies, 44–45
customer value propositions, 117–118,
  121–122
cycle, turnover, 171–173

Dell, 48, 195
demographics, 7–9, 74, 168
Dendrite, 156–157
development, *see* engagement (of talent)
Development Dimensions International,
  158
Dice Inc., 23
differentiation strategies, 40
dimensions, 158
diversification, 37–38

divisional organizational structure, 94
division of labor, 61–62
Dokken, Wade, 197
dot-coms, 5, 23
Doubletree Hotels Corporation, 156
downsizing, goal of, 80
Drucker, Peter, 88
    on knowledge workers, 10, 11
    on personnel management, 234
DuPont, 36
duration, turnover, 171–173

East Alabama Medical Center (EAMC),
    120, 158–159, 174, 204–205
eBay, 29
echo boomers, 7
e-cruiting, 153–154
efficiency, recruiting, 216–219
efficiency strategies, 41–43, 47, 50, 68
e-learning, 194–196
electronically-aided performance manage-
    ment, 188
Electronic Arts Inc., 160, 162, 163
EMC, 156
Emerson Electric, 147
employees
    in alumni relationships, 176–179
    business competencies residing in,
        71–72
    commitment level of, 59–60
    loyalty of, 164
    personal career responsibility of, 72–73
    talent market value of, 187
    temporary, 82
    turnover rates for, 164–165
employer-of-choice initiatives, 124–130
employment branding, 123–124
employment marketplace(s), 5–6, 12–13
    emergence of, 68–70
    internal vs. external, 108
    shifting power in, 73–74
    transparency of, 108–109
    see also talent flow
engagement (of talent), 15, 182–206
    development vs., 183
    learning opportunities for, 193–199
    measurement of, 221, 223–224
    as more than "being there," 182–183
    overlap of talent flow processes and,
        183–185
    performance management for, 185–193
    processes related to, 100, 183
    replacement of commitment/loyalty
        with, 80–83
    rewards systems for, 199–206
Enron, 44, 189, 190, 191, 211

environmental employment factors, 129
equity participation programs, 202
Europe, 9
evaluation, see scanning
executive teams, consensus on strategies
    in, 30
external scanning, 107–112
    in business strategy management cycle,
        51
    of current and projected markets for tal-
        ent, 107–108
    of external talent market, 108–109

Fannie Mae, 105, 119
Fast Start initiatives, 185
Fayol, Henri, 63
Federal Express, 92, 118
Fenwick & West LLP, 129
The Fifth Discipline (Peter Senge), 41
financial measures, 209–211
financial services companies, recruiting
    costs at, 151
Fiorina, Carly, 189
Fisher College of Business (Ohio State
    University), 4–5, 146
focus strategies, 40
forced distribution performance manage-
    ment, 191–192
forced-ranking processes, 188–192
Ford, Henry, on history, 34
Ford Motor Company, 36, 62, 189, 192, 195
Fortune 100 companies, downsizing at,
    189, 191
Fortune 500 companies, 82, 154
Fortune magazine, 118, 119, 120–122
Frank Russell Company, 157, 158
free agents, employees as, 72–73
functional organizational structure, 94

gain-sharing programs, 204–205
Gallup Organization, 157
General Electric (GE)
    alternatives to financial measures at, 210
    annual human resources review at, 101,
        104
    forced ranking at, 189, 190, 191
    personal career responsibility at, 69
    shorthand strategy at, 50
General Motors, 36
generational nature of talent, 79–80, 107
generation X, 80, 128–129
generation Y, 80
generic strategies matrix, 39–40
Genesys Software Systems, 192
Gensler, 178

Gerstner, Louis, 117
  on IBM as marketplace-driven company, 45
  on vision at IBM, 34
Glenroy Inc., 187
Gloudeman, Tom, 143, 192, 236
Goodnight, Jim, 140
goodwill, 10
Goodyear, 195
Grant, Robert, on elements of business strategies, 33
great places to work initiatives, see employer-of-choice initiatives
Greece, 9
growth-share matrix, 38
Gulf & Western, 37

Hackett Best Practices, 137, 172, 196
Hamel, Gary, on people as asset, 3
Hammer, Michael, 48, 96, 97, 101
Handfield-Jones, Helen, 233
healthcare sector, recruiting costs in, 151
Herman Miller, 119
Hertz, David, 198
Hewitt Associates, 201
Hewlett-Packard (HP), 48, 189, 190, 195
high-tech sector
  as fuel for wider economy, 167–168
  recruiting costs in, 151
Hire.com, 161
hiring manager satisfaction rating, 216
historical measures, 213
Hopper, Grace, on strategy measurement, 208
horizontal alignment (of objectives), 136–137
HP, see Hewlett-Packard
HR, see human resources
The HR Scorecard (Brian Becker, Mark Huselid, and Dave Ulrich), 18, 235
human capital wealth, 11
human relations concepts and practices, 65
human resources (HR), 3, 5
  and awareness of human capital obstacles, 90–91
  business processes and organization of, 98–99
  business processes facilitated by, 101
  and business strategy communication, 145
  credibility of, 14
  current opportunities for, 6–13
  future opportunities for, 13–19
  ownership of talent strategies by, 234–239

"silo" organization of, 97–98
views of, 14–15
Huselid, Mark, 18, 235

IBM, see International Business Machines
IBM Global Services, 81
industry trends, 166–168
Information Technology Association of America (ITAA), 4, 5, 14
information technology (IT), 4–5
  and decline of pyramid hierarchies, 68–69
  talent required for, 70–71
information transparency, 148
initiatives
  and alignment of objectives, 136–139
  in building talent strategy, 130–140
  mapping, 133–136
  and measurability of objectives, 136
  setting/choosing, 130–132
In Search of Excellence (Tom Peters and Robert Waterman), 41
insurance organizations, recruiting costs at, 151
intangible assets, 10, 11, 29
integration strategies, 35–36, 45–46, 48
internal scanning, 91–107, 110–112
  in business strategy management cycle, 51
  of competencies, 91–93
  of organizational structure, 93–96
  of talent processes, 96–103
  of talent resources, 101, 104–107
International Business Machines (IBM)
  core competencies at, 92
  customer needs/strategy merger at, 45
  employee responsibility for careers at, 69
  mission and vision of, 117
  solution strategy approach at, 78
  vision at, 34
Internet economy, 211
IT, see information technology
ITAA, see Information Technology Association of America
Italy, 9
ITT, 37

J. Walter Thompson, 177–178
Japan, 9
jobs, simultaneous creation and elimination of, 80
job security, 66–67, 69
Johnston, Susan, on EAMC performance dimensions, 159
Jupiter Media Metrix, 153

Kaplan, Robert, 211–212
Kelleher, Herb, 140
Kirkpatrick, 221
Knight, Charles F., 147
knowledge, talent as, 74, 77
knowledge component (of work), 77
Knowledge Universe, 11
knowledge workers, 10, 11, 77

labor, division of, 61–62
Lands' End, 143, 192–193, 196, 236, 237
layoffs, 80–81
Layoff Tracker, 25n.9
leadership
    brand, 10
    success and mind-set of, 115
    and turnover, 169
    turnover of, 82
learning
    measurement of, 221, 223
    for talent engagement, 100, 193–199
    and turnover, 169
Life Themes model, 157
Litton, 37
Lockheed Martin Information Manage-
    ment Services, 163
long-term employment, 66–67
Love, Geoffrey, 189, 191
loyalty, 80–83, 164

management cycle(s)
    for business strategies, 50–57
    for talent strategies, 88, 89
management science, 37
Manpower, 82
manufacturing, 10
mapping (of objectives and initiatives),
    133–136
market alignment (of objectives), 138–139
market-facing talent strategies, 18–19
marketplace, employment, 12–13
Marshall, S.L.A., 163, 164, 165
Maxwell, David, 105
McKinsey & Company, 13–15, 82, 104, 120
measurement(s), 208–230
    balanced, 211–213
    cost-benefit analysis as, 224–230
    electronically-aided, 188
    financial, 209–211
    of learning, 221, 223
    of objectives, 136
    operational, 211, 214–224
    of performance, 185–186
    of performance management processes,
      223–224
    process, 209–211

for recruiting, 214–217
of retention/turnover, 217–222
strategic, 211, 224–230
of talent engagement, 221, 223–224
of talent flow, 214–221
of value creation, 209
Michaels, Ed, 233
Microsoft, 189, 192
Miller, Gail, 157
mind-set, talent, 140
Minnesota Mining and Manufacturing,
    119
mission statements, 116–117, 119
models (business strategy), 33–45
    competency, 40–41, 47, 49–50
    customer, 44–45
    efficiency, 41–43, 47, 50
    integration, 35–36, 45–46, 48
    planning, 37–38, 46, 48–49
    position, 39–40, 46, 49
    shorthand, 43–44, 47, 50
Monster.com, 153–154, 174, 177
Moore's Law, 29

Navistar, 195
net present value (NPV), 226–227
New Economy, 11
new hire quality rating, 216
Nike, 118, 195
Nohria, Nitin, 189, 191
Nortel, 48, 195
Norton, David, 212
NPV, see net present value

objectives, 130–140
    alignment of, 136–139
    in building talent strategy, 130–140
    mapping, 133–136
    measurability of, 136
    setting/choosing, 130–132
Ohio State University, 4–5, 146, 201
100 Best Companies to Work For, 120–122
operational measures, 211, 214–224
Oracle, 195
organizational structure, scanning of,
    93–96
Organization Man and Women model, 58–
    61, 64–65, 68, 235
The Organization Man (William Whyte),
    58–60, 65, 74
orientation, 184
ownership of talent strategies, 87, 233–239

Parkview Medical Center, 187
Patagonia, Inc., 49, 118, 120, 122, 143
Perez, Becky, 161

performance management, 185–193
electronically-aided, 188
and employee's stake in talent market value, 187
and forced-ranking processes, 188–192
as information sharing with employees, 187–188
infrastructure basics for, 192–193
low opinion of, 186–187
measuring processes of, 223–224
for talent engagement, 100, 185–193
performance recognition, 169
personal credibility, 144
Personnel Decisions Incorporated, 187
Peters, Tom, 41
PicturePeak, 198–199
planning strategies, 37–38, 46, 48–49
population changes, 7–9
Porter, Michael, 39–40, 143
portfolio-planning strategies, 38
Portugal, 9
position strategies, 39–40, 46, 49
Powertrain Group, 186–187
The Practice of Management (Peter Drucker), 234
predict-and-prepare strategies, 37
preferred employers initiatives, *see* employer-of-choice initiatives
PricewaterhouseCoopers, 187
process measures, 209–211
process-reengineering initiatives, 70
Procter, Harley, 123
Procter & Gamble, 123
productivity, 9–12
birth of, 62–63
estimation of, 185–186
of integrated knowledge work, 77
product markets, competition in, 71
products (as important to customers), 78
project/product/process matrix structure, 95
Prudential Financial, 160–162
pyramid hierarchies, 64–67, 68–69

Rainmaker Thinking, 80
Ray, Rebecca, 143–144, 196–197
recruiting, 153–163
competencies used in, 154–159
e-cruiting for, 153–154
efficiency measures for, 216–219
measures of, 214–217
spending on, 149–153
as talent flow process, 99
talent flow strategies for, 153–163
and talent relationship management, 159–163

reemployment, 176–178
reengineering, 96–97
Reengineering the Corporation (Michael Hammer and James Champy), 96
relating (as talent flow process), 99
relational employment factors, 129
relationship strategies, 109, 148–149, 159–163
reserve military forces, 108
retention bonuses, 202–203
retention (of talent), 163–179
and alumni relationships, 176–179
in comprehensive talent strategy plan, 166
and employee turnover rates, 164–165
and good vs. bad turnover, 169–171
influences on, 166–169
as integral part of talent flow strategies, 172, 174–176
measurement of, 217–222
as talent flow process, 99
talent flow strategies for, 163–179
and turnover cycle/duration, 171–173
return on investment (ROI), 224–226
rewards, 199–206
customization of, 200–202
as influence on turnover, 169
for talent engagement, 100
Ritchie, Kelly, 236
ROI, *see* return on investment

Saratoga Institute, 164
SAS Institute Inc., 122, 172, 174, 203, 204, 217, 218
SBUs, *see* strategic business units
scanning, 91–112
of competencies, 91–93
of current/projected talent markets, 107–108
external, 107–112
of external talent market, 108–109
internal, 91–107, 110–112
of organizational structure, 93–96
preliminary assessment summary for, 110–112
of talent processes, 96–103
of talent resources, 101, 104–107
scientific management movement, 62–63
Senge, Peter, 41
SEP (single enterprise program), 195
service markets, competition in, 71
services (as important to customers), 78
Session C meetings (GE), 104
75:75-boundary rule (Cisco Systems), 43
shorthand strategies, 43–44, 47, 50

SHRM, *see* Society for Human Resource Management
"silent generation," 80
simple organizational structure, 94
single enterprise program (SEP), 195
small-group integrity, 163–164
Smith, Adam, 61
Society for Human Resource Management (SHRM), 6, 146, 151, 186, 187, 201, 216
Society of Personality and Social Psychology, 168
solution strategy approach, 78
Sony Corporation, 92
Southwest Airlines
  business-level competencies at, 92
  business strategy of, 49
  as customer service provider, 78
  customer value proposition at, 117–118
  mission statement of, 119
  as one of 100 best companies to work for, 122
Spain, 9
spending
  on learning/training, 193–194
  on recruiting, 149–153
Staffing.org, 151, 215–216, 217
staffing services industry, 149, 150
Standard Oil, 36
strategic business units (SBUs), 17, 48
strategic measures, 211, 224–230
strategy(-ies), 15–18
  business, *see* business strategy(-ies)
  talent, *see* talent strategies
  as term, 35
strategy-level competencies, 93
strategy objectives matrix, 131, 132
Sun Microsystems, 189, 190

Taco Bell, 147–148
talent
  as competitive advantage, 70–71
  customer value provided by, 78–79
  generational nature of, 79–80
  history of, 60–73
  as knowledge, 77
  as organization asset
  survey of what is important to, 126–128
talent flow, 15
  measurement of, 214–221
  processes related to, 99–100, 148–149
  replacement of commitment/loyalty with, 80–83
  and talent engagement processes, 183–185
talent flow strategies, 142–179
  alumni relationships in, 176–179

  building retention into, 172, 174–176
  communication of, 145–148
  e-cruiting as, 153–154
  getting basics right in, 144–145
  incomplete sets of, 143
  for recruiting, 153–163
  for retaining talent, 163–179
  signature successes in, 143–144
  and spending on recruiting, 149–153
  talent competencies used in, 158–159
  and talent flow processes, 148–149
  talent relationship management as, 159–163
talent gap, 4
talent-learning initiatives, 196–198
talent markets
  current/projected, 107–108
  external, 108–109
talent mind-set, 140
talent readiness assessment, 105–107
talent relationship management (TRM), 159–163, 227–228
talent resources, scanning of, 101, 104–107
talent strategies, 18–19, 87
  building, 118–140
  and business strategies, 88, 90–91
  components of, 116–140
  definition of, 88
  determining content of, 91
  financial impacts of, 214
  management cycle for, 88, 89
  measures of, 210, *see also* measurement(s)
  overall process related to, 88, 90–91
  ownership of, 87, 233–239
  value of, 115
  as works in progress, 142
  see also specific topics
talent value propositions, 116–118, 120–123
talent wars, 12–14
tangible assets, 10, 11
technologists, 11, 77
technology, 28–29
temporary workers, 82
Texas Instruments, 179
Textron, 37
time metric, 216
to-do lists, 114
top-down strategies, 51
total shareholder return (TSR), 223
Towers Perrin, 73, 81, 200
transactions, delivery of, 144–145
TRM, *see* talent relationship management
TSR (total shareholder return), 223
Tulgan, Bruce, 80

turnover
    cycle/duration of, 171–173
    factors influencing, 166–169
    good vs. bad, 169–171
    measurement of, 217–222
    as norm at leadership levels, 82
    rates of, 164–165

Ulrich, Dave, 18, 235
United Parcel Service (UPS), 195
universities, 177
University of Michigan, 144
University of Southern California, 168
UPS (United Parcel Service), 195
U.S. Census Bureau, 7, 77, 82
U.S. Department of Labor, 171–173
U.S. military, talent reserve concept in, 108
U.S. Military Academy at West Point, 133

value, 10, 16, 115
value creation, 209, 213
value propositions
    customer, 117–118, 121–122
    talent, 116–118, 120–123
valuing talent, 58–83
    and administrative science, 63
    during business strategy eras, 68
    and commitment/loyalty vs. talent
        flow/engagement, 80–83
    as competitive advantage, 70–71
    and customers' definitions of talent
        value, 78–79
    and division of labor, 61–62
    and emergence of employment market-
        place, 68–70
    and employees' responsibilities for own
        careers, 72–73
    and end of pyramid hierarchies, 68–69
    and fragmentation of work, 65
    and generational nature of talent, 79–80
    historical perspectives on, 60–73
    and job security, 66–67, 69
    as knowledge, 74, 77

and level of employee commitment,
    59–60
in long-term employment with internal
    career opportunities, 66–67
and possession of business competen-
    cies, 71–72
prior to division of labor, 61
and pyramid hierarchy of companies,
    64–67
and scientific management movement,
    62–63
variable reward plans, 201–202
Vault.com, 124
vertical alignment (of objectives), 137–138
vertical integration, 45–46, 48
virtual integration, 48
virtually integrated business structure, 95

Wal-Mart Stores, Inc., 49, 92, 119
"War for Talent" report (McKinsey), 4, 82,
    104, 115, 233
Waterman, Robert, 41
The Wealth of Nations (Adam Smith), 61
Web-enabled performance measurement,
    188
Web technologies, 194–195
Welch, Jack, 140
    business strategy of, 50
    on forced ranking, 189
Welch, Lynda, 163
West Point U.S. Military Academy, 133
Whyte, William, 58–60, 65, 74, 235
William M. Mercer Inc, 186
work
    fragmentation of, 65
    knowledge component of, 77
workforce turnover matrix, 170
working for, belonging to vs., 59–60,
    82–83
work-level competencies, 92
World at Work, 201, 202, 204

Yahoo!, 29, 43
Y2K, 5